Al Jackson, Owner,

JADE WRITING

Huáng
黄
Yellow

Tíng
庭
Court

Jīng
经
Classic

Individual Phase Space User Manual

D1415111

JADE WRITING

Huáng   Tíng   Jīng

黄　　庭　　经

Yellow　　Court　　Classic

Individual Phase Space User Manual

Translated by Imios Archangelis and Miaoyu Lanying

Edited by Imios Archangelis

JADE WRITING

  经

Huáng   Tíng   Jīng

黄   庭   经

Yellow   Court   Classic

Individual Phase Space User Manual

Publisher: Avatar Solutions Inc.

December 2010 Edition

ISBN: 978-1456481650

Translation: Imios Archangelis and Miaoyu Lanying

Editing, Introduction, and Commentary: Imios Archangelis

Proofreading and Technical Editing: Corinne Chaves

Design: Sanela Kruskic

Web site: http://jadewriting.org

Copyright © 2010 by Imios Archangelis, All Rights Reserved

No parts of this book may be reproduced or utilized in any form or by any means, electronic or mechanical, including photocopying, recording or by any information storage and retrieval system without written permission of the publisher.

Dedicated to the Peace and Prosperity of All

DISCLAIMER

The meditative and other self-development or healing techniques described in this book should not be attempted without the supervision of a qualified teacher, or adequate prior experience. The ideas and opinions expressed in this book are intended for general philosophical insight only and should not be used for prevention, treatment, or curing of aging or any disease or to replace any religious belief. Please contact your health care professional or qualified spiritual guide for direct personal help or guidance. Neither the publisher nor any person who participated in development on this book shall be liable for any direct, indirect, incidental, special, consequential, or punitive damages resulting from interpretation or the use of the text.

ACKNOWLEDGEMENTS

The editor would like to express deep gratitude to his past and present personal teachers and instructors:

Vera, Vukadin, Horlin, Silvano, Nika, Aliona, Gaon, Elisabeth, Leah, Gary, George, Hermes, Manuel, Freya, Lu and Chen,

to his beloved Muse: Snowy Qi Moon, and

to many friends for their love and support and to the authors of the wonderful literary work who helped him build the system of knowledge that he is now passing on to others in the present book.

Contents

Editor's Preface

The present text has been developed from the personal notes of the editor, Imios Archangelis, collected during his study of the original Yellow Court (Huang Ting) manuscript and the related alchemy practice, with an invaluable help of the editor's Chinese language teacher, Miaoyu Lanying, and his friend, Taoist practitioner Corinne Chaves.

The explanatory notes and comments thus reflect the editor's opinion and practical conclusions regarding subject, and may not be always authoritative in the field. The contemporary interpretation of the mystical subject is presented in hope and attempt to be valuable for everybody, but in the spirit of "open source software": suitable, for the original purpose of the "developer", but not guaranteed to work for others (as every person is unique, with the own theory about Universe), without adaptation.

To maximize efficiency in passing the information, a direct experience (tested from various angles, through years of study and practice) is used whenever possible in this work. The rational speculations, matters of faith or assumptions (not founded on experience, or *seeing* of the specific scenery), are hereby reduced to the minimum. To get familiar with the reference framework and the operational concepts used in the study and the interpretation of the main text, it is recommended to read the Introduction first.

Some relatively thorough explanations of the selected esoteric topics are provided, with the hope of bringing this ancient mystical teaching closer to a wider circle of readers. The vocabulary and analogies of the popular science, as well as the selected systems of the mystical knowledge, are used in an attempt to provide a truly multidimensional, unbiased view. However, by their nature, even highly perfected philosophical (and all rational) views can aspire to penetrate, at best, only a half of the actual reality. For the other, practical half, the personal efforts to interpret and intuit the inexpressible are necessary, preferably supervised by an experienced, authentic teacher. The Taoism as well as other Internal Traditions clearly separate these two planes of the individual cultivation.

Due to the depth of the subject, the intended audience for this text includes mature, educated, and open-minded persons who are self-motivated to understand the secrets of the Universe and of themselves and to apply them for the Good of All. In the Hindu tradition, this path of cultivation is called Jnana Yoga (the Way of Direct Knowledge). In Taoism this is a Path of the Scholar-Warrior. The followers of the other paths, such as Bhakti Yoga (The Way of Love or Belief), can also find an inspiration here (the editor also has a deepest reverence for the Divine, ancient author(s) of the Huang Ting Jing and accomplished masters of any tradition). However, their main venue of individual accomplishment would more likely be in the line of direct intuitive alignment, accepting the guidance from the chosen enlightened guide (e.g. from Guru in Hindu or Nagual in Toltec tradition, a priest of person's religion etc.).

Due to the limits of the translators' knowledge, the vastness of the topic and difficulties in the interpretation of the lexical compositions from the 3rd Century, some hidden clues given by the ancient authors could be missed in the translation. To present more accurately the treasure of the original text as well as to give the opportunity for readers to create their own unique interpretation, the original Chinese characters, their Pinyin transliteration, and literal English word-by-word translations are provided. Chinese characters of the original text are shown in large typeface, to enable the study of their visual patterns. In the editor's opinion, even after thousands of years of transformation, they still contain deep archetypes of meaning (or, according to the "Jade Writing" terminology, the embodiment of the high "spirits") encoded in their geometry (in the similar manner as the old Qablistiic texts wrap the inner meaning in the hidden numeric series). The original plates (now artwork in the public domain) of the great 4th century calligrapher Wang Xizhi are also provided in the Appendix.

Most of the Chinese words in the commentary are presented with Pinyin Romanization (as the Ruby text over the characters), to make them more familiar to the Western readers. On the other side, translators chose not to adopt or develop a full English terminology for the core Chinese concepts of alchemy. In the spirit of the pragmatic discussions on the topic, the frequently used Chinese terms were referred to by their widespread English equivalents (rather than precise Pinyin) that are later described in a Glossary.

The terms Tao, Tai Chi, and Qi are used for 道 (Dào), 太极 (Tài Jí), and 气 (Qi), for instance, as it is difficult to find simple but adequate translations for the ideas they describe. Such terms have really become part of the continuously developing international vocabulary, similar to the word "geometry" that originated from the Greek, "algebra" and "alchemy" from the Arabic, or "Waltzer" from German.

In editor's experience, a pragmatic utilization of the various vocabularies and philosophical systems is rarely easy, but it can be well worth the invested effort, in a similar way as the integration of the various programming languages and system libraries to the software project. Even though the theory and practice of Taoism is amazingly deep and every other knowledge system mentioned is also whole and beautiful by itself, each of them also has some unique powers (analog to different renaissance arts or weapon expertise in Kung Fu) that can help the practitioners to efficiently address some specific issues. Deep, true principles, regardless of their expression means or tradition, are always in accord.

According to an old Chinese proverb 天人合一 (Tiān Rén Hé Yī) (Tian Ren He Yi), all Heavenly People are in Harmony as One. Both inner and outer conflicts are basically born from the lack of true knowledge and understanding. Sharing of the secrets of Nature, that we Individually discover, can stop suffering and help All. When people are confronted with a difficult challenge (like one posted by the original "Jade Writing" text), every bit of wisdom could make a crucial difference.

Introduction to the Jade Writing Practice

The "Yellow Court Classic" (or "Jade Writing") is a part of one of the three divine manuscripts of the Taoist Immortality Cannon, which were, according to legend, written by the mythical sovereigns of the legendary Three Purity realms[1].

Yuan Shi (元始, meaning "Original Truth"), wrote the "Scripture of the Magic Jewel" (Yuan Shi Jing or Ling Bao Jing), that postulates the laws of the Primordial Existence, where no separations exist.

Ling Bao (灵宝, meaning "Spiritual Treasure"), wrote the *"Great Cavern Scripture"* (Da Dong Jing), that contains the present original text, "Yellow Court Scripture". His writing defines various interplays of the polarities (Yin and Yang), from which the most prominent ones are represented as Macrocosm and Microcosm.

Dao De (道德, meaning "Tao and Virtue"), whose incarnation was Lao Zi, wrote the famous "Scripture of Tao and its Virtue" or "Dao De Jing" (probably better known as "Tao Te Ching" in older, Wade-Gilles transliteration). This scripture explains the philosophical and ethic principles of the Human Life as a part of Nature.

While the manuscript attributed to the Grand Purity Realm ("Dao De Jing") has been translated into English many times, this is a first attempt to fully translate the "Yellow Court" manuscript, associated to the Supreme Purity Realm, even though it has been vastly popular in ancient China alchemy practice and referenced in many later classics written by high authorities on the subject, such as "The Secret of the Golden Flower" by Lü Dong Bin.

---

1) The three purity (三清) worlds of Taoist Heaven are Jade Purity (玉清), Supreme Purity (上清) and Grand Purity (太清)

Lady Wei Huacun (魏華存), from the Highest Purity (上清) tradition of Taoism, received this manuscript through a mystical channel and introduced it as one of the core texts of the school. In the year 288 C.E. Ge Hong, a famous alchemist and collector of mystical texts, made the first known written record of it. The first preserved transcript (the plate photos included in the Appendix) was done by the famous Wang Xizhi, "The Sage of Calligraphy" (303-361 C.E.). The real author and age of the manuscript are not known, but according to the text itself, it was composed (as a Void, rather than physical, formation) by the emperor of the Highest Purity Realm, Ling Bao himself.

The manuscript consists of the two parts, or sceneries, of the human existence, External (high-level) and Internal (detail view), which are sometimes used independently. The External (Wai) Scripture has 100 verses in 3 chapters and is fully contained in the more comprehensive Internal (Nei) Scripture of 435 verses and 36 chapters. The verses of both scriptures are composed of precisely seven words. The traditional titles of these scriptures are "External Scenery Scripture of the Yellow Court" and "Internal Scenery Scripture of the Yellow Court". The unifying title, mentioned in the text itself, is: "Jade Writing".

"Jade Writing" exposes the philosophical view of the place of an Individual Being within Universe in a great depth. Its underlying concepts and metaphors draw from the ancient systems of knowledge that are, in modern times, often considered naïve or superstitious. According to the editor's understanding, such perception is far from the truth. The same objective reality is described today in a different language, based on modern scientific postulates, syntax, and semantic rules; however, the use of different expression formulas or the style doesn't make the old statements inaccurate.

The practical philosophers of ancient times spent an enormous time and energy trying to understand nature and themselves and were able to successfully intuit very deep secrets. A quote from the "Yellow Emperor Medicine Classic" describes this fact as: "Not so long ago there were people known as achieved beings who had True Virtue, understood the Way of Life, and were able to adapt to and harmonize with the universe and the seasons. They too were able to preserve their awareness and energy through proper intent." The preservation of the Individual energy and spirit through the cycles of change, mentioned in the quote above is a pretty common cultivation target in Taoism, referred to as the Longevity or (at the higher stage) *Immortality*.

One of the main differences between modern and ancient or esoteric sciences is in specialization and isolation of the functional domains versus generalization of applicability and the holistic approach. While modern science is usually very efficient in providing explanations that cover the specific, well defined, fields and conditions, its highest and most general theories unavoidably meet the "gray zones" between the areas of expertise and *singularities* in the scope of validity. There are many reasons for that. Artificial boundary conditions between the domains, relatively arbitrary choice of the initial postulates, limitations of the observer-observable and cause-effect pattern are some of them.

On the other side, the "sleeping beauty" of semantic richness (coming from a more fundamental "Object Model", which continually deals with the "Theory of Everything") of the ancient knowledge systems is often veiled into either intentional proprietary "encoding" or unintentional ambiguities. Their precious truths are difficult to convey in terms of the usual human language. Mystical teachings, each in its own terms, usually define a system of questions, rather than answers. Every being holds an existential secret, a singularity of black/white hole within, a true root of the equation of the own life. In depth understanding of ancient wisdom generally requires much more effort and overall dedication than modern science and it is a never-ending process that continues from one challenge to another.

The hidden treasure of the ancient systems should not ever be underappreciated or given up though, as it can provide some much-needed help regarding existential (holistic health, overpopulation, continuity of consciousness etc.) and moral issues (as meaning of life or personal place in the world) that present a challenge to old and new societies alike. Its hidden light never goes away and bursts in the dreams or the random inspirations of even most rational people, driving inventions that benefit the life of mankind.

To support the scientific understanding of the theory described in the "Jade Writing", this Introduction provides a cursory overview (barely scratching the surface of such an immense topic) of some of the key concepts of the ancient text in the light of modern science and couple of other esoteric traditions.

Lü Dong Bin[2] (呂洞賓) provided one of the clearest brief definitions of the Tao that says: *"Tao is that which exists through itself"*. This incredibly deep insight (that applies to all entities that *embody* Tao) can be directly related to modern physics and theories of "spin" and "symmetry preserving transformations". We can observe the underlying principle everywhere in nature, from the rotation of the stars and planets down to the oscillations of superstrings. The physical rotation holds the substance of inorganic bodies together, the *circulation*[3] of water in the nature has been

---

2) Editor's favorite saint, one of the Chinese "Eight Immortals", featured on the title page of this book. The "Yellow Court Classic" / "Jade Writing" actually was not a direct part of editor's lineage teachings of the "Complete Reality" school, however its study was propelled by the thought: "If Lu Dong Bin himself used this scripture in his practice, it must be something really good".

3) The circle and oval or its 3D equivalents: sphere and egg represent a primary form of existence, as in medieval, magic-square formula: "Sator Arepo Tenet Opera Rotas" (God Preserves Its Creatures through Rotation). The concept of "Ouroboros" (or negation of the negation) of Western alchemy also is a symbol of the living Nature.

the basis of the life formation, while the circulation of life energy in the body gives birth to the consciousness.

Science most often considers the "spin" attribute of physical entities as a passive *property* (e.g. an electron happens to have "spin 1/2" or "our planet revolves around Sun in 365 days"), rather than as the *cause* of their behavior. However, that begins to change as we see that oscillation, "spinning", of superstrings *creates* the forms of higher elementary particles (such as quarks, electrons, and protons). David Bohm's "holonomy" law also describes the generation of quantum objects from themselves as the *"new wholes"*, in the process of *"continuous becoming"* where the change (similarly to the concept of "Yi Jing", the "Book of Changes"), rather than a form or substance, is a constant.

Ancient and esoteric systems often postulate that any well-defined exercise or ritual, carried out with a repetitive engagement of the *will*, such as a Karate Kata, a Tai Chi form, or a meditation protocol, truly *creates* a new, more advanced existence of the practitioner. By following or inducing the purposeful cycles in the own body, nature, or spirit, an individual is able to qualitatively *enhance* personal existence without pulling anything substantial from the outside environment. This paradox (practically all the deepest laws of Nature are paradoxal) cannot be expressed by analytic equations of energy conservation, i.e., in the scope of the symmetrical relationship between the macro-cosmos and micro-cosmos, as the whole process originates and ends in itself. However, internal sciences do offer a descriptive, but unambiguous, explanation formula, in which a fifth, central and quintessential, element ("Earth" in Chinese or "Akasha" in Indian and Western practice) collects the essence or *information* formed through an interchange of the four phases of the repetitive pattern.

Taoist philosophy especially operates with the above concept, and extends it to a *continual cultivation* paradigm. Cultivation in Nature, according to Taoist thought, never ends, and even the beings who have achieved immortality continue to overcome the own weaknesses and enhance personal integration with the Tao. In other words, cultivation is orthogonal and *asymmetrical* in relation to the paired concepts of the ordinary world. An apparent contradiction that "Divine does not develop as such development would be in conflict with its absolute perfection" can be ruled out by a paradoxal insight that cultivation *is* perfection, i.e., one of the dimensions of the Divine (mentioned, commonly assumed, contradiction holds only if the concept of the perfection is seen only from one side, as an attribute, but not from the other, as the action or the *Word* of the God).

A system, such as a living being, that is closed and, at the same time, open to the structural change, could be, in modern terms, described through somewhat special *ultimate symmetry*, composed of both standard "spin" *symmetry* and its adjoined, organically complementary *asymmetry,* or symmetry-breaking "dimension". These two modes of reality, that can be presented as joint, but independent logical axis, complement each other, as Yin and Yang of Tai Chi, the Great Ultimate. Entities, that are subject to such symmetry, manifest through the pairs of the complementary (symmetrically mapped) domains, the transcending (symmetry-breaking) domain and the neutral cross-point (or pivot point) where all three domains intersect, constituting a symbolic T-Cross formation (as in "Lotus Palm Hands" posture, where horizontal palm symbolizes Yin and vertical palm Yang), as on Figure 1.

A description of the structure of the Universe based on three constituents has been basis of the multiple philosophical theories, such as the mentioned Taoist theory of Three Purities, Hermetic Emerald Tablet ("What is above is the same to what is below, to accomplish the wonders of One Thing"), the geometrical composition of the space (comprised of semantic triangles) by Greek philosopher Plotinus in his work Enneads) or the combinatory definition of the space developed by the modern physicist Roger Penrose (as three-state nodes of the spin networks).

Development

Asymmetry
(Transcendence)

Polarity 1 | Polarity 2

Crosspoint

Symmetry

Figure 1: True/Tao Cross or Totality Centering (TC) Symmetry

In addition to the rational, deterministic behavior on the "horizontal" line (that represents a plane where the "polarity" laws of the ordinary symmetry are projected upon), this composite configuration allows definition of the other, very interesting transformations, such as the exchange of the essential roles of the polarities, in a seemingly paradoxical manner, e.g.: "to give is to receive" or (a quote from the present ancient text): "difficulties and problems to which we are exposed by going along the noble way, will turn into benefits when the phase changes".

A prominent Taoist concept of 无为 (Not Doing or Wu Wei)  is deeply related to a beneficial changes of environment or *scenery* around the *invariant center,* so we would refer to the overall principle as *Tao Cross* (or briefly TC) *symmetry.* One of the most important principles, that could be efficiently presented using this concept, is the relation between the point and a space that contains it, or the element (or subset) of the set (domain) and the set as the whole. For the

19

Individual awareness such interconnection can be described as *Totality Centering*, a continually cultivated holographic *Oneness* with the Great Divine Spirit of Universe without, around the root of the *Uniqueness*, a Divine Spark, within.

In the materialistic science (and daily life routines) we are mostly dealing with the natural laws on the "horizontal" (symmetry) axis, while the ever-increasing *contextual awareness* of the discoveries could be associated to the "vertical" axis of the Figure 1.

Even though a context-specific recombination of scientific facts to achieve operational goals is widely used by the modern technology, a pre-requisite *knowledge-dependent system of reference* is rarely considered as an "organic", indivisible aspect of the phenomena. However, the quantum physics do take this factor into account by necessity (through the deterministic balance between individually unconstrained energy and spatial data), in its definitions of the wave functions of elementary particles.

Information is also regarded as the viable physical entity in the theory of the reversal of super-entropy (peak information density) "black holes" into "white holes" in the formation of supernova[4] stars (that could also be considered as a type of the mentioned "TC transformation"). The law that relates energy and information is often intuitively expressed in the formula (more precise than is usually assumed) "Knowledge is Power". This simple folk wisdom has been silently driving the development of many people throughout ages.

---

4)　A record about sacrifice and resurrection of the Christ (a Unique manifestation of the One God) manifests the same Heavenly Law as "Entropy Crossover" of Supernova. This pattern is also recorded in the Post-Heaven and Pre-Heaven arrangements of 8 Trigrams (Ba Gua), or in the structure of the Qabalistic Tree of Life, where 5 lower Sephirots are displayed in the shape of Cross (symbolizing a separation of the opposite elements), while the upper 5 Sephirots are in the formation of Upper Pentagram Star (symbolizing the reintegration of elements in a flow according to its True Nature).

While TC Symmetry can be related to any system (Galaxy, Star, Planet etc.), one of its especially interesting specializations, related to the Individual accomplishment and *Living Ascendance* (that replaces usual crossovers during death and birth), is thoroughly researched in Taoism and the some other mystical traditions[4] and is presented as *"Identity Enhancement Symmetry"*, on the Figure 2 below:

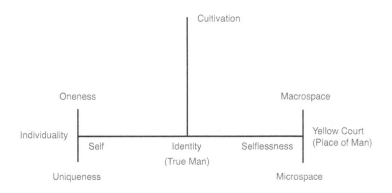

Figure 2: Identity Enhancement (IE) symmetry

Here we can see a composition of the two TC symmetries into one, the first one defined around Existence (or the Being, symbolized by number 1) and the second defined around Void (Non-Being, symbolized by number 0). A single higher symmetry (around the central point and vertical axis) designates a continually evolving *Identity* as a transcendent abstraction of Existence and Non-Existence.

An asymmetrical development and enhancement towards the higher perfection is built upon the symmetries, established in the combinatory space of a temporal (Post-Heaven) Chaos. This pattern is, in editor's opinion, very beautifully abstracted by the inspiration formula from Bible: *"It is God who arms me with strength and makes my way perfect"*. We get the strength of our arms, the "flying wings" and the charge to do things from the matching pairs of polarities comprising specific symmetries of the rational

21

world. In the orthogonal, spiritual, dimension, we reach the experience of the primordial peace, the state of perfection that rises between the polarities of the each cycle.

The *holographic inclusion* of a more fundamental law in the specialized principles is in place here. So, both existence and non-existence "nodes" manifest the same TC symmetry as the root "node", but also feature "drill down to detail" of the more specific planes. The sequence of such holographic property inheritance develops within both (mutually balancing) Impersonal (Cosmos, Selflessness) and Personal (Body, Self) Nature of the Individuality, indicated as the right and the left axis on the Figure 2.

According to the first chapter of 道德经, "The Book of Tao and its Virtue" by Lao Zi, the Cosmic Polarities (Heaven and Earth), are founded around invariant Non-Existence or Void (number Zero, the neutral element for additive group of the positive and negative numbers). This Void opens a space, a range of possibilities, for the Existence (number One, the neutral element of the multiplicative group that contains infinitely small and large numbers) of the myriad "things".

Chinese characters for Person 人 (Ren) and Wizard 巫 (Wu) curiously also manifest single and triple T-Cross geometry of the Figures 1 and 2. Archetypes or "spirits" that correspond to the ancient characters often impart deep meanings and virtues through the patterns of its form.

Character Ming (名, meaning "name" or "place"), according to Tao Te Ching, is a common, unnamable "root" for both Existence and Non-Existence, similarly as the program variable can become zero or one. In more detail levels of symmetry, a series of the polarity pairs (such as Hyperspace and Space, Cosmos and Earth, Planet and Person etc.) that enhances the *potentials* of the root can be developed around Non-Existence. In a similar way, an infinite balanced series of the *manifested forms* takes shape in the Existence.

A series of potential states and behaviors of any system in physics is described by its *phase space*, while in the software development all possible behaviors of the program are specified by the *source code* of the computer runtime application. Every person forms a vision of what she or he wants to be, within the currently operational existence. This new self is continually converging towards some ideal (even though such target can be superficial, implanted by a social routine). A true place of any Being lies in the *active present*, between the achieved and the new self, past and future. Living beings develop their genetic code by exposure to the environment and by learning from the adult, or more advanced specimens. At the level of Consciousness, a number of the Archetypes of the Collective Wisdom[5] are supporting the development of every Individual. Its true source, in a pure form (which is gradually revealed through methodical meditation efforts) is assumed to be Divine, and the basis of *Alchemy* ("Al" meaning God in Arabic), whose other part ("Chemistry") is up to Individual Human efforts.

According to the traditional interpretation of the ancient text of "Jade Writing", all potentials of the human form can be learned and integrated by contacting the related intelligent *carriers*, the *spirits* in charge of the specific functions, forms, organs etc. (who are like angels of the Western traditions or programmers who maintain the specific blocks of the code). Such view is difficult to accept in the modern world, as every being is considered a separate unit, with a fixed form. However, if we adopt the idea of the co-existence of the closed (separated, unique aspect) and open (oneness, holistic) aspect of the holographic sub-totalities (hereby related to the sentient beings of different form), the mentioned type of inter-change is much more logical.

---

5) A concept introduced by famous psychologist C.G. Jung, particularly in his work "Archetypes of the Collective Unconscious". It indicates the informational templates (like mythological characters, processes, goals, etc.) that human beings inherit from the collective and follow, without necessarily being directly taught about them or aware that they are using them.

Similar process of the development of abilities of any living organism is, according to modern science, driven by its genetic program. The system of the co-operating structural conscious archetypes of the mystical view hereby is matched by different patterns or routines of the genetic code. As the creation of that code is affected by the living circumstances, the overall personal genotype program is also self-modifying and extensible. However, modern human biology is directed more towards the treatments of the diseases, not a development of the human potentials, so the operations of Internal Alchemy, or "code updates" which affect the current organism (rather than just next generations), are not yet a subject of the mainstream study. In editor's experience, both or these views, personal (of a mystical art) and impersonal (scientific), are contained in some higher symmetry. One or another description could prove to be the more practical in the specific circumstances or the stage of the personal development. It is more important to pragmatically utilize and extend the Individual "Phase Space" and thus enjoy the fuller life.

Most of the mystical and religious frameworks agree that in the spiritual development of every Individual, the helpful attitude towards the other beings, mercy and goodness are the core of any virtue. According to Taoist teachings though, the Outer world can be actively supported most thoroughly *from within* by the perfection of the Internal space first. A practitioner is able to radiate good deeds within the own operational field, at the level in which he or she can reproduce the image patterns[6] of the (understood, adopted and integrated) higher archetypes, similarly as the Moon reflects the light that comes from the Sun.

Such "Work for Heaven", that aspires to bring some subtle Virtues from Above to the Manifestation, gets naturally

---

6) Shàng Dì
    上帝, Divine Forefather, Archetype of the all Archetypes or Virtue of the all Virtues is the Taost concept closest to the Western idea of the One God.

balanced by the *ascension* of a fulfilled individual spirit to the celestial existence. This is experienced as a relatively coherent Presence (according to a level of the personal integrity), though which one can circumvent default dissolution of awareness between incarnations. The growing tree of implications, related to the possible elements and transformations of this framework, is too vast to be analyzed here, but one well-known paradigm from Taoist philosophy conveys its core principle: "Tao Te Ching" says: "One come from Tao, Two comes from One, Three comes from Two and the whole world comes from Three". One, Two, and Three stand here for the three mentioned Taoist Purity Realms: Jade, Highest and Greatest Purity respectively, along with their sovereigns. Realms and their representatives denote impersonal and personal aspect of the specific Divine archetype: Heaven, Earth and Individual or Undifferentiated Origin – Wu Ji (as One), Supreme Polarity – Tai Ji (as Two) and Harmony of Three Treasures (as Three).

In the terms of earlier symmetry definitions[7], "One" would correspond to an asymmetry (vertical) axis, while "Two" and

---

7) Of course, similar concepts can be found in the other deep metaphysical teachings (as the human interpretations of the objective, silent Truth):
    • Myamoto Musash begins his "Book of Five Rings" by addressing the Heavens (standing for Jade Purity), Buddha (Highest Purity), and Bodhisattva Kwan Yin (Greatest Purity).
    • Hindu philosophy mentions "Three Steps of Shiva" and the first Buddhist Patriarch in China, Da Mo, created "Sanchin Kata" around the three steps and subsequent return to the beginning.
    • Teachings of Hermes Trismegistos define Creator, Cosmos ,and Man divinity
    • Genesis/Old Testament discusses the Original Paradise, Tree of Knowledge, and Tree of Life (matching the descent from Jade to Greatest Purity), while Christ in the New Testament claims, "I am the Life, the Truth and the Way" (indicating the reverse, return path from Greatest to Jade Purity, back to the embrace of the Divine)
    • Mesoamerican Toltec teachings define concept of Tonal (first perception - Man), Nagual (second perception - Earth), and Total Freedom (third perception - Heaven), also matching the ascension/return path through the realms of the Three Purities.

"Three" could be mapped to the pairs of symmetries balanced around the center, at any level.

Jade Purity: "One" (— Yi) or "Great One" (太一, Tai Yi) represents the undivided oneness (continuum is often symbolized by the jade stone, due to its coherence and smoothness), governed by Yuan Shi (whose alternative, ancient name was Tai Yi), the emperor of the Primordial existence, Creation and Originality. Typical meditative experiences regarding this plane can come as responses to a question: *"Who am I"*. The answers are of course very subjective, but usually related to the integration of the archetype of Truth, spiritual completeness or Primordial Oneness (Wu Ji) with the Tao. The categories of internal and external, space and time do not exist on this plane.

"Two" defines "Supreme Purity" and the highest, Yin/Yang polarity, governed by Ling Bao (meaning Spiritual Treasure), the ruler of the richness of the variety and wisdom. In modern system theory and genetic science, the related principle is a constant re-combination of existing elements to generate new qualities, capabilities, "plenty". This process is in no way degenerative (as the intentional discord of a completed wholeness is), it is just a different type of primordial state that adds some new order within (like the Star in Cosmos) or the *polarization of the continuum* (by TC-transformation) into Pre-Heaven and Post-Heaven, Inside and Outside, Past and Future. Yang "view" from without (Pre-Heaven or spirit between incarnations) is transforming to the Yin "view" within (Post-Heaven, or the incarnated soul) and vice versa, around the axis of the immutable primordial wholeness (this dynamics is often symbolized by the infinity sign). A related meditation could be: *"What am I"*, a continuous flow of the "re-alignments" between micro-cosmos and macro-cosmos or between the current state of existence and anything we can be, our Self and Selflessness. Number Two and the subsequent even numbers, according to ancient teachings, correspond to the formation of Cosmos, Earth, or our Aura in the Universe. The

"Yi Jing" (The Book of Changes) uses the numeric base two to explore and predict varying states of Nature.

"Three" defines the "Greatest Purity", ruled by Dao De (or the "Lord Lao", one of whose incarnations was Lao Zi), who is considered to be a Master of the Triple Separation (similar to Hermes Trismegistos in Western Alchemy), of Three Dan Tian ("elixir fields" in head, heart, and abdomen), and Three Treasures (Jing: essence; Qi: energy, vitality; Shen: spirit), teacher of the re-integration of the living being into new, higher forms of Harmony (He), through alchemy. Yet another polarization of wholeness occurs at this level[8]. Primordial Unity and the Supreme Duality are here reflected and integrated within the Individual Being, Yin and Yang are mapped to a personal Jing and Qi (or Water/Substance and Wind/Energy) and Wu Ji to personal Shen (a limitless Spirit). A crude software systems correspondence could consist of (initially default) Data (for Jing), Program Code/Flow (for Qi) and Programmer (for Shen).

The object of meditation here would be the *"Life"*, an uninterrupted flow within the physical existence, an ongoing transformation process that re-integrates all diversities, like the water cycle[9] in nature. Clouds, as the subtlest form of water in its cycle (often mentioned in the "Jade Writing" and other alchemical texts), symbolize Yang aspect of Water (Jing), that is crucial for the alchemical transportations. The sea of energy or body essence (on the bottom side of the imaginary axis that connects above and below), provides a fuel for the "water wheel". The Qi flow, similar to the Wind (caused by temperature difference) in the Nature is often symbolized by the animal like a tiger, on which Immortals ride. Qi flow induces a "water wheel" or the *Cultivation* process (often symbolized by the Tao sign) from which new

---

8) The body (or personal subspace) center, lower Dan Tian, is initially formed around a nucleus of the primordial cell of life, then enhanced by the growth of additional energy flows and self-awareness.

9) As in Tabula Smaragdina of Hermes Trismegistos.

"incarnations" of the Individual Spirit (Shen) emerge. Lao Zi has been considered the creator of innumerable life preservation and enhancement methods. Odd numbers traditionally signify an active force, and the number three presents a numerical base for the teachings of the 81 chapters of "Tao Te Ching".

The Emperors of the Three Purities are generally presented as Yuan Shi in the middle (timeless creation), Ling Bao on his right (young man, void, potential), and Dao De (Lao Zi) on his left (old sage, individuality). The sequence of "Sun", One to Three symbolizes the path of Heaven, or the "God loves me" process, through which the three treasures of Tao are generated and an Individual comes to maturity. Three to One symbolizes the rejuvenation, the return path of Earth, Moon, or "I love God"[10], where the three treasures[11] are re-integrated in the new, unique way, in the process of the personal contribution or an "Internal Alchemy". A continuous cultivation circle, or changes of the *Great Oneness* (Tai Yi), comprised of the Receiving of the Divine (powers along with challenges) and the subsequent *Great Work* with every bit of energy and consciousness, balances itself through the formation of the *Individual Void* or the *Capacity for Love*.

This process[12] enhances a *Virtue* of the Divine Tao (道德), a Void that balances Existence, where the peaceful *seat* (or

---

10) Or everything that is Divine, according to a character of the individual: love of the Truth or knowing true self (following "Gnotti Saitum" message of the Apollo's temple in Delphi), loving the Beloved (as beautifully depicted in poems of Rumi) or world, work for the Good, or any other action from heart. It is important here that in the practitioner's attitude no manifested form should replace or parallel the Divine, as it is just an island in the vast sea.

11) Symbolized on this book cover: clouds stand for created essence, tiger represents Qi, Lu Dong Bin—accomplishment of True Spirit.

12) "Yi Jing" (Book of Changes) defines meaning of cultivation in the comment of the first Hexagram: "True Man Works with the Forces of Heaven to Cultivate Virtue".

the true place) of the practitioner can be found and preserved. Its silence is hidden in the center (*Zhong He*, the core of one's being) of the never-ending process[13], where the gifts of the continuous creation are honored by its dedicated use for the Divine purposes (such as action for general good, sincere love, and discovery of Truth).

Editor's Tao teacher often says that "Tao is the Way of Living". The mentioned living exchange with the world is independent from any naming conventions or rational interpretation[14] and can be found anywhere in the Nature (in Cosmos with the laws of Relativity on one side of the spectrum and elementary particles and superstrings on the other). In our physical existence, the life flow can be noticed in the simple act of breathing in and out through all pores, feeling how light comes (from Oneness) into the body and Dan Tian (Uniqueness) and then flows back. Mentally we can register how archetype[15] behaviors manifest in our life patterns (as on Figure 3). Physical and mental symmetry elements finally merge and transcend along the open line of eternal cultivation, into our *True Nature* (Zhen).

The overall process of the exchange between Oneness and Uniqueness has been a topic of considerable research in different sciences. The great German philosopher G.F.H.

---

13) Unlike the cycles that repeat on the same level in "samsara" sense, continuing process here indicates "Raising on the Planes' in always new, mysterious steps. Even Divine energy works along this path, according to the Bhagavad Gita, while individual beings follow.

14) The nameless, heavenly, principles are crucial, so an alchemist from the other system of knowledge might use terms: Ain Soph, Ain, and Ain Soph Aur (for Jade, Supreme, and Grand Purity) or equivalent with the same internal effect.

15) Here we extrapolate the concept of archetypes (in addition to their application to a domain of collective consciousness, introduced by C.G. Jung), to include the more generic informational matrix that patterns the behavior of the whole Nature by defining possible manifestation forms or the phase space of its various sub-totalities.

Hegel thoroughly described the combined diversification and unification process in his books "Science of Logic 1-3", where his first and second (Objective and Subjective) laws of logic correspond strongly to mentioned patterns of receiving and giving Love or Light (even though his third step leans toward abstract concepts, rather than our objective but personal integration of Cultivation and Peace into Tao). The materialistic dialectic theories, on the other side, postulate the ordinary (personal or group) human desires (one side of the polarity, the aspect of recombination and growth, but also of Chaos) instead of pragmatic, but cultivated spirit (an "Elevated Man" of the "Yi Jing") as the target of the dialectic synthesis. As metaphysical sciences work in paradoxes,

Figure 3: Three Purity Archetypes (Tai Yi, Tai Wu, Tai He) replicate freely in many unique beings capable of centering (Zhong) them.

the Individual elevation though cannot be ever truly accomplished on the account of other beings (as in some Nietzsche's interpretations), but is based on goodness, mercy, virtue and the invariance towards peer rewards.

A modern quantum physicist, David Bohm, has also contributed to a very deep understanding of the natural analysis and synthesis. He describes its patterns as the "unfolding"(symbolized by Two) and "enfolding" (symbolized by Three) of the holo-movement continuum.

The described symmetry of the Three Purities provides an archetypal root of the varying forms of individual existence. To achieve the balance, every enhancement (manifested in pairs of polarities) needs to be balanced by understanding and re-integration (synthesis, "Three"), to avoid dissipation. "Totality Centering" process however doesn't end with the Individual spiritual realization of oneself. According to ancient teachings it actually requires that one "forgets" the own enlightenment and *become* rather than just *know*. Steps along the spiral sequence: 1-2-3 need balancing with the steps 3-2-1, a return path to the Primordial, as on Figure 4 below:

INDIVIDUALITY

UNIQUENESS   ONENESS

UNIQUENESS x ONENESS =
INDIVIDUALITY

Figure 4: The Return to Tao and its dimensions

31

On the above re-draw of the unknown ancient original, the cranes (that were, according to other paintings, mystical carriers of the flying Lao Zi), symbolize reintegration on multiple levels, the variations (walk) of One (Tai Yi). The six steps (1-2-3-3-2-1) correspond to Six Lines of "Yi Jing". The first three steps correspond to a lower Foundation Trigram, the establishment of the Individual form, the "Hidden Dragon", the period of study and "spin" from the inertia of teachers. The last three lines (and return steps) correspond to a higher Trigram, own Accomplishment and the "Flying Dragon" state, where three Dan Tian of the practitioner "spin" out personal variety and enlightenment.

The basis for all steps is the single Hexagram line, matching a Primordial Circle[16], or the "Walk of One" (Tai Yi), in four phases. In the inorganic world, the projection of this concept to a horizontal plane can be simply a circle in a complex frequency space or a "world line" recorded by oscillations in Nature, for instance of electromagnetic wave traversing through space (riding on the "switch of the polarization planes" of the electric and magnetic field)[17].

In the world of living beings (where each of the listed axis is more complex, enfolding the three-dimensional space into one line) we can observe *evolution* (development in time) of the archetype (set of potentials) of the species (vertical axis) based on the continuous knowledge acquisition by the specific specimens (axis of Uniqueness) and the refinement of the common genetic program (axis of the Oneness).

For the beings that cultivate consciousness, the axes are aspects of the Individuality. After integrating and understanding some principle (or his or her body form), the

---

16) Mathematic concept for this could be Circle, "S" or SO symmetry.

17) The "Rotary Magnetic Field", conceived by the inventor Nikola Tesla, is also based on the cross-conversion of mechanical, magnetic and electrical field and used everywhere in modern society to obtain the alternate current electricity.

practitioner can initially operate it in isolation or for the own needs. However, when the knowledge matures (along the Uniqueness coordinate), he or she needs to embrace the world with open arms (Oneness axis) and merge the own achievement with All, in every action, moving with the Earth and Cosmos. Finally, in the intersection of Uniqueness and Oneness, in a pragmatic application of the inner values, a mystical Individuality[18], rises between the own Unique Development path and the Selflessness, with its own *Light*[19]. In the third stage, practitioner operates in a similar way as a small *Star*[20], where the Uniqueness is associated to the Star sphere, the Oneness to its light rays (merging, in action and experience, with the Cosmos) and the Individuality to its Mystical Rebirth at the Primordial level, which connects it to a Divine. The internal treasures achieved with these three aspects are Jing, Qi and Shen, respectively. Every accomplishment of the above three steps corresponds to one metaphysical re-integration with the Void, a nameless Virtue and Potential, represented on the picture above as the waves of the body of the Dragon on whom the practitioner flies to Tao.

In a simple practical sample, a basic memorization of some Tai Chi form movements can correspond to a first level of achievement, its integration with the whole body and external applications to the second, and its performance

---

18) Taoist often refer to these steps as Moonlight, Sunlight and Mystical light. Similar dimensions of the development can be found for instance in Toltec teachings, as Tonal, Nagual and Third Perception, or, in the tradition of Golden Down in Student, Adept and Magus achievement levels.

19) It is interesting that the letters of the Hebrew world Avr, comprised of the letters Aleph Vau and Resh and the corresponding Tarot cards: Fool, Priest and Sun correspond the a similar principles we mentioned: isolated richness, selfless spreading of the words of wisdom and self-sustained light.

20) "Every Man and every Woman is a Star" claimed Aleister Crowley in his "Book of the Law".

from the "Inner Source", without mental or physical activity to the third level. Each integrated form (or mastered body function) comprises a metaphysical "spin" of the dimension of an Individual into Oneself. Only the individual *form* and the *experience* ("what" and "life") of the practitioner are affected by the transformation process, while the identity ("who", the subject of the action)[21] stays immutable.

Even though nothing substantial is "added" to a practitioner, a new potential is achieved and can be also passed, by example (or pure information induction), to any being who is able to adopt the same "virtue", so in that way, a master can help his students. The process of the spiritual development is beyond Space and Time, in the realm of Truth.

True People (真人, Zhen Ren), according to a terminology of ancient Taoist texts, such as "Jade Writing", are the Beings who are part of the Truth. Any man or woman has potential to raise to that level, where the physical form is based on the personally generated wave energy and there is no death.

The term 子 (child or son, also associated to a beginning of the new cycle of the daily circulation of the five elements), which can be seen throughout this book, symbolizes the above elementary circle of accomplishment, of the specific function by the ordinary Human Being along the cultivation path. This is a new whole that emerges (in the "center of the circle") as a target of the cultivation, in many varieties. Each of these circles embeds, in a holographic way, the Nature of the whole Universe, a loop of Time into itself. The Tao practitioner would work on a number of such circles (based on the own capabilities and affinities) which would all merge

---

21) "Who am I", "What am I" and "What is Life" are some of the basic koans (similar to questions in Chan and Zen Buddhism) in the meditative practice of the "Intensive of Enlightenment, introduced by Charles Berner (Yogeshvar Muni), a great technique to develop the direct knowledge and seer abilities.

to an integral system, along the path of the Individual[22] accomplishment.

The *Immortal Embryo* (胎 仙, Tai Xian) is a term used in Taoist alchemy for an initial, organic integration of the set of such elementary functions of the overall human being, which advances towards the Truth. This Embryo nourished by a Great Harmony (Tai He) of Nature in the Center (Zhong He) is an incorruptible internal foundation for a continuing Individual growth. It eventually matures to a self-sustained being at the different level of existence (Zhen Ren).

The main alchemical laboratory where the transformation takes place, according to ancient Tao scriptures, is the own body. The elementary circles of change provide a blueprint for the different physical functions of life (such as breathing, blood circulation, eating, thinking, communicating etc.), blending together into the overall personal "phase space".

Old alchemists were intensively studying, as well as practically utilizing and optimizing, the rhythm of natural periodic functions that comprise such space or "keep the body together" (neurological waves, breathing, blood pulse, metabolism and others)[23]. "Jade Writing" describes in detail the Taoist view to such organization of the human body, and its relation to the external world (as duality on one side and reintegrated whole on the other) along with the governing principles, laws or *spirits* of such interrelationship.

---

22) Ancient Taoist Masters didn't forgo family life, but considered children and support to them as an act of selflessness, an extension of the cultivation process (made possible with a surplus Jing and Qi) along the line of Oneness, but not the substitute for the own, eternal, Unique Mission or Individualization.

23) Western Quantum physicists, such are Erwin Schrödinger in his work "What is Life" and, even in deeper detail, Milo Wolff in his concept of "Wave Structure of Matte" in the work "Schrödinger's Universe" also supports view that everything in Nature can be understood much better if we think about standing wave oscillations, rather than a solid mass.

An understanding of the inner processes described in the scripture and a subsequent application of the acquired knowledge should, according to the ancient author, bring great health and longevity benefits and even immortality to the practitioner. If we assume that the (previously described) concept of the Universe based on *continuous creation and transformation* is correct, there are no obvious logical contradictions that would constitute an inherent (i.e. "heavenly") impossibility[24] for such a goal to be achievable. While the science today most often studies closed systems in nature (i.e. no external inputs or outputs) as they provide good analytical abstraction for the most cases of common interest, the uniqueness of the world at any moment[25] (as well as the meditative experience and research) point out that such picture is sometimes too simplistic. In reality the information ("software"), that underpins the overall behavior and possible reactions of a living being, is in the process of a constant upgrade (while the *intent* of its functionality, matching the spirit of Earth and the center, Yi, is preserved).

Even though dedicated efforts of mind and body are necessary to thoroughly embody wondrous mystical laws of Universe[26], it is said that even the plain repetitive recitation of the scripture (which has powerful sound rhythm and melody when read in Chinese) by a practitioner will bring great health benefits.

---

24) Practical difficulties in making memory or life invariant through Tao Cross transformations are immense, but "Yi Jing" says: "True man has to make sure not to oppose the laws of heaven, while the obstacles of earth are just ordinary mountains and abysses".

25) Expressed e.g. through "Panta Rei" ("Everything Flows") proverb of Heraclites

26) The ancient principle of "Yang chasing Yin", or "Mind over Matter" practically means a gradual upgrade of the own genetic program (by internally generated Jing, rather than using only the one obtained by inheritance), similar to modern experiments where scientists have successfully created synthetic live cell

"Jade Writing" postulates a clear interconnection between a principal biological functionality of the human body and its connections to a spiritual world, thus resolving a gap (common to the modern thought) between the abstract world of mind ("design" of our own world) and the physical existence ("implementation"). The maturation of the mutual support between these two seemingly separate spaces enables metaphysical re-integration (point of peace) of the related (indivisible in reality) aspects of the Individuality.

The five major organs of Traditional Chinese Medicine (liver, heart, spleen, lungs and kidneys) are referenced as the seats or centers of the "breath" (pivotal, peace points) of the five main body Spirits. The term *Yellow Court*, or the central hub,[27] refers here to the element (agent) of "Earth" (Spleen organ) which coordinates the other elements ("Wood" on the East , "Fire" on the South, "Metal" on the West, "Water" on the North). Even though the spleen is not considered very important by the Western Medicine, in Taoism it has the central role of the incorruptible ruler that initializes, harmonizes and synchronizes the work of his subjects according to well-known Taoist "Wu Wei" concept[28].

The book inter-relates many aspects of the roles of the Five Elements, the Five Organs or Phases. A basic assumption is that the five functions of the internal organs are driven by the nature and intent of the governing externally[29] hovering

---

27) 中 (Zhōng): middle, center of Heavenly Peace as foundation of change. Yellow Court is also any space (Dan Tian, Spleen or whole body) where cross-over of the Spirit to Body or Body to Spirit occurs.

28) 无为 (Wǔ Wéi): non-doing, avoid personal reaction to change, let Heaven act spontaneously (1-2-3 steps of the new circle of IE symmetry), after we did all we can (3-2-1 steps).

29) In Toltec Shamanism, there is a similar concept of the external Nagual, that also aligned to the incorporated Nagual aspect. In the Bhagavad Gita, the internal (unique) spirit is also to be "conquered" or pacified by external, Spirit (Universal, Oneness).

spiritual aspect of the Primordial Existence of the Individual. The functions of the five spirits are elaborated consistently throughout the text, and can be associated to the specific gradients of the periodic functions that operate inside the human body:

a) Metal, Lungs, the Po spirit "descends from Heaven to an Abyss" (matches gradient of the tangent at the far left, or -180 degrees on the graph on Figure 5)

b) Water, Kidneys, the Zhi spirit, collects the water and weight at the lowest extreme, doesn't ascend or descend (tangent at -90 degrees)

c) Wood, Liver, the Hun spirit, "ascends from Earth to Heaven", cultivates growth (tangent at 0 degrees)

d) Fire, Heart, the Shen spirit, neither ascends or descends, it rules or flies at the top (tangent at +90 degrees) of the specific domain

e) Earth, Spleen, the Yi spirit, descends again, but "to asymmetrical dimension", storing all "flavors", or experience, collected throughout the "spin" cycle (tangent at +180 degrees)

The subtle functions of five elements (descending, collecting, ascending, ruling and transmuting) do not always flourish spontaneously and need to be cultivated (transformed through TC transformations) like sprouts, out of the five gross (stressful) energies: grief (in Lungs), fear (in Kidneys), anger (in Liver), overexcitement (in Heart) and restlessness (in Spleen).

"Jade Writing" also describes various mutual relationships of elements, mostly through the personified combination of clothing (red for Fire, yellow for Earth, white for Metal, black for Water and green for Wood). As in Traditional Chinese Medicine we can see here mutual support (Sheng) and restriction (Ke) cycle. Grandchild support principle, for

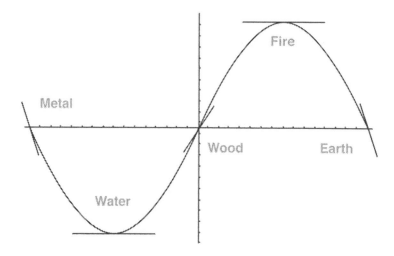

Figure 5: Sample Internal Periodic Function and the Five elements

instance (mentioned in Chapter 2.20), indicates that[30] in
restriction cycle, stability of grandfather element profoundly
influences behavior of the grandchild element, for instance:

- Strong personal growth (Wood) controls restlessness
  (Earth)
- Inner balance (Earth) controls leaks of personal energy
  (Water)
- Inner power (Water) restrains over-zealous personal
  mind (Fire)
- Enlightenment (Fire) of one's Unique identity controls the
  attachments of the body (Metal)
- Strong body (Metal) channels personal growth (Wood)

While the study of the functionality of the Three Dan Tian
centers and five organs is probably most prominent, the
ancient text also describes other types of structural systems
of the body and its relation to the Universe. The other two

30) Following a pattern similar to the Western "Banishing Ritual of
     Pentagram", also a typical pattern of a Primordial Circle.

important *odd* numbers (seven and nine) referenced in text are also not picked by chance, but according to the structure of the 9x9 table (also mentioned in Chapter 25 of the "Yellow Court Internal Scripture") on the Figure 6 below:

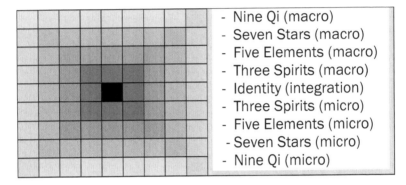

- Nine Qi (macro)
- Seven Stars (macro)
- Five Elements (macro)
- Three Spirits (macro)
- Identity (integration)
- Three Spirits (micro)
- Five Elements (micro)
- Seven Stars (micro)
- Nine Qi (micro)

Figure 6: 9x9 square: center, 3 spirits, 5 elements, 7 stars, 9 Qi

This table (presenting different definitions of the Yellow Court concept) can be considered a composite of the central cell surrounded by squares of three, five, seven and nine cells in a sequence, corresponding to Hui Yin, three Dan Tian and Bai Hui circumference respectively. It also matches four iterations of the gnomon[31] based squares in the Pythagorean geometry, the number of orbits in the atomic shell[32] and other independently discovered patterns[33] that describe a fairly pragmatic structure of the integration of an Individual into a surrounding space.

---

31) The gnomon is the base unit of building so called "figurate" numbers that extend towards corners (in this case 1, 1+3, 1 + 3 + 5 etc.)

32) The electron shell, around atomic nucleus, is structured into one s-orbit, three p-orbits, five d-orbits, seven f-orbits and nine g-orbits

33) Like 9, 7, 5, 3 and 1 ring, assigned to the various Archetypes of the Conscious Beings in the Tolkien's "Lord of the Ring" series or the same pattern in Qabalistic writings of the Abremaline the Magus.

This integration is accomplished through the five spirit fields: nine-fold Yi (Integration, spirit of the Earth), seven-fold Po (Animation, spirit of the Metal), five-fold Zhi (Will, spirit of the Water), three-fold Hun (Intellect, spirit of the Wood) and the unique personal Shen (Mind, spirit of the Fire) in the center. The individual understanding and integration with the Universe through the converging external circles (nine to one) into the center of the self is balanced by a radiance (one to nine) of the selfless inner light to the world.

This nine times nine formation also represents another, greater[34] role of five elements, where previously mentioned five gradients have place in the middle (5-cell) circle, and serve the three high spirits (often mentioned in the text) of the second (3-cell) circle (also associated to Three Dan Tian), in the regulation of the core body metabolism.

Number seven represents the next level in the process of the externalization of body functions (following five organs): seven senses, seven sensory openings in the head and seven directions around the body[35]. Cosmically, the number seven is associated to the seven stars of the Big Dipper constellation (as on Figure 6). While the numbers one, three and five are related to inner space, the number seven refers mostly to a border between inner and outer space.

Seven sensory openings (along with the acupuncture points, that match 365 days in a year) represent the crossover (TC symmetry) junction passes between macro-cosmos (stars or spiritual source of the all energy and life) and micro-cosmos ("earth patterns", internal organs), time and space, so adepts who have the knowledge to regulate the energy flow (by integrating specific spiritual energy into the inner field through meditation, massage, acupuncture etc.) through these gateways have the "keys of their own kingdom".

---

34) That can be associated to Taoist Greater integration or Western Greater Pentagram Ritual.

35) "7 rays" towards front, back, left, right, up, down and center.

Most people do not regulate their sensual interactions, so their Qi easily gets attached to the external (post-heaven) objects and leaks out (resembling the radiation of energy that happens by releasing the electrons from the f- shell of an atom). The process through which the "external light" of stars and spirits turns to "internal light" (energy) of the body organs and vice versa is not abrupt or linear, but happens along the curve of gradual change, in a similar way as the

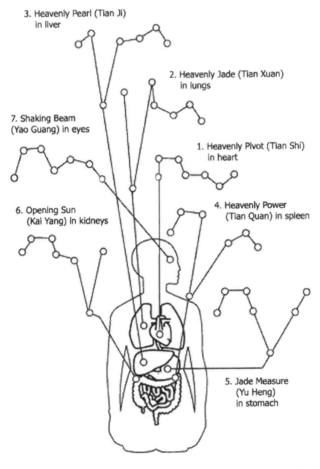

Figure 7: Projection of 7 Big Dipper Stars in Human Body

physical penetration of electromagnetic waves into different surfaces, i.e. logarithmic[36] in nature.

The number nine is related to the external, "soaring" field of the individual. The Figure 7, as well as the simplified illustration of the ancient Immortal Pathway scroll on Figure 11 shows the connection of the body to heaven through a "Nine Peak Mountain", representing nine Qi or mental rhythms that drive the body functions.

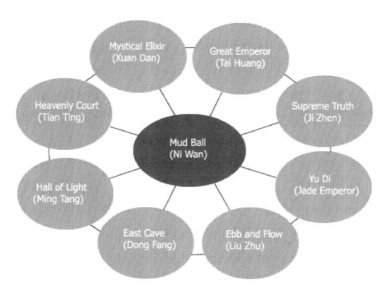

Figure 8: Nine Palaces of Brain (9 Mountain Peaks, 9 rhythms)

Only "one peak", or one ninth of brain functions and external field is generally used (similarly as very few elements in nature have filled the g-shell of their atom). In analogy to the five directions on the two-dimensional surface and seven directions in the three-dimensional

36) log(1) = 0 as change to peace, log(0) = random, change (of peace). Here hides also a connection between the frequency and time domain (ν = 1/t), and the logarithmic function (1/x is a derivative, change function of log(x)).

space, in this circle there are the nine directions[37] (or rather modes) of the four-dimensional reality.

While the configurations corresponding to smaller odd numbers were points, lines or surfaces, here we see the full three-dimensional "worlds" and their leading spirits, arranged around an invariant center, the Ba Gua forms of change in the spiral flow of Time. The usual focus of the awareness is concerned only with one or two of these worlds (the present moment and the time flow in a physical world).

The energy configurations based on *even* numbers are also described in the "Jade Writing" (as well as in other mystical Taoist texts). Complementing the transformative nature of the odd number formations, structures based on even numbers constitute a steady, deep *potential* between the polarities (like positive and negative, heaven and earth, sun and moon), through the geometrical arrangement in the shape of *borders* around a mystical center. These borders or separators, make a foundation for the seclusion of central point from the surrounding infinity (through its multi-dimensional aura). Two points (symbolizing Yin and Yang) form the pillars around the central point in the one-dimensional space (line). Four sides (symbolizing Four Seasons) surround the central point in the two-dimensional space (plane). Six surfaces (symbolizing six directions or six healing sounds) constitute a cube around central point in three-dimensional space and finally (as mentioned above) eight spaces (matching Eight Trigrams or Ba Gua) make a hyper-cube around the central point in the four-dimensional continuum. At higher dimensions, the overall surrounding actually consist from gateway elements of all previous dimensions, i.e. surface point is bordered by four lines and four points (yielding another form of Ba Gua structure), while

---

37) Nine bodies of change (also studied in the Nine Star dynamic Feng Shui): Tao Body stays in center, while eight Ba Gua are time-shifting body states from full Truth (Qian) to full Mystery (Kun) and back, in a Tao Cross transformation between the two moments of time.

there are totally 26 border elements around spatial central point (six surfaces, twelve lines and eight points).

In a similar manner we saw the analogies between the 9x9 table and the structure of the electronic shell of the atom (in space-curving configurations matching the odd numbers), we can notice here a remarkable correspondence between the structures of the eight trigrams of the "Yi Jing" and the eight quarks of the atom kernel, based on pairs of "flavors".

The even-number structures, with its origin in the Highest Purity (associated to dualities), in addition to its separation function, serve as magnetic poles or gate pillars which direct and guard the living flow within. Choosing the right "batteries" and poles of the living potential (e.g. points as "detached dedication", "good and better", "truth and mystery" or "external alchemy of West and internal alchemy of East", instead of less productive "good and bad", "depression and hyperactivity", "suffering and excess joy", "judging others" and "criticizing oneself") is essential for everyone's energy, even outside of the world of alchemy.

Note that *ontologically true*, or Pre-Heaven polarities (Highest Purity polarizations of Oneness, such are Heaven and Earth, left and right side of the body, Soulmates in True Love, teacher and students, two photons in quantum entanglement etc...) are continually re-generated and refreshed by the underlying power of creation (Jade or Original Purity) behind, thus providing reliable source of inspiration and energy for the ongoing spiral cultivation of the practitioner. Polarities formed in Post-Heaven (i.e. manifested world), such are two poles of electromagnet, or society induced desires and objects of desire, on the other side, are formed through the "manual" addition of an external energy (i.e. electricity) of its domain. An intuitive practitioner can easily feel the difference between such energy of "car battery" and one of the remote "hydroelectric power plant". Plain battery can output only the post-heaven energy that has been invested into a separation of polarities and requires a continual re-charge to keep it operational.

Different paths of cultivation integrate various formations of polarities and the matching re-integrations that follow, thus enabling different potentials of the Individual Phase Space.

The Totality Centering (Tao Cross) symmetry of the space of the Individual transformation (that keeps one's Identity invariant) is, according to "Yi Jing", a subject to the six lines or two trigrams of the hexagram of change and can be (according to previous discussions) analytically represented by the following formula:

[1]   Ic(enh) = [TC] Ic = [TCm] [TCs] Ic

or

Ic(enh) = Dm [To x Tu] Ds [Tu x To] Ic

where   Ic = Original Identity (circular) symmetry
        Ic(enh) = Enhanced Original symmetry

        TC = Totality Centering / Tao Cross Transformation
        TCm = Totality Centering in Manifestation direction
        TCs = Totality Centering in Sublimation direction

        Dm = Duality Crossover (Manifestation, Ext -> Int)
        Ds = Duality Crossover (Sublimation, Int -> Ext)

        To x Tu = Oneness to Uniqueness Transformation
        Tu x To = Uniqueness to Oneness Transformation

By performing the overall transformation in the own spirit, body and the field of action (good deeds), in a unique "Great Work", a practitioner, aligning with the Universe, *develops a higher (consciousness preserving) symmetry* than ordinary Living Being and records the new information to a "Book of Heaven" or the Virtue of Tao, her or his true *Jade Writing*.

The ancient Taoists also had a physical tool (in addition to "Yi Jing" patterns) to represent the Universe "In the Ball", the Feng Shui Compass. The Compass displayed on the

Figure 9 below is comprised of the six transformations of the initial Four Season / Five-Element Primordial Circle:

Figure 9: Feng Shui Compass, featuring six transformation rings

The constituents of the Three Inner circles (associated to Figure 3), comprised of 8 Trigrams, 24 Mountains and 72 peaks, are structured by multiplication of the number four (4x2x3x3). Each of these circles has a very deep meaning in the Taoist tradition, similar to the transformation steps of the Western Alchemy. The identity of one's Primordial Circle at the beginning and end of all steps is, of course, immutable in the process, similar to a Philosopher's Stone. The Eight Trigrams circle represents the eight directions in the world and the Eight Extraordinary Pre-Heaven Qi Vessels in human body, the basis of all our thinking and actions. The initial multiplier of Two yields the Dm symmetry of the First TC transformation, the mentioned Heavenly "summersault" of the Spirit to Manifestation. The further ternary, 3x3 transformations ("Yi Jing" defines 9 as the number of Heaven), represent a "rain" of the Heavenly Riches on Earth (mapping to the usual nine repetitions in Taoist Practice).

The structure of the Three Outer (corresponding to Figure 4) Circles, comprised from thirty six, twelve and four elements (72/2/3/3), maps the road back to the four-fold Primordial Circle and the Four Palaces (East, South, North and West, each hosting the respective seven positions of the Big Dipper in the Sky). The initial divider of Two here designates the Earthly Ds "summersault" of the Body (or the World) back to the Spirit, the merge of Self into the Selflessness, through the meditation and the work for Oneness. The 3x2 transformations (bringing 72 back to 12), associated to a number of Earth (6) by Yi Jing, are also frequent in the Taoist practice and symbolize the return to center. The number twelve is associated to a number of Earthly branches, the signs of Chinese Zodiac and the Acupuncture Channels where Post-Heaven Qi flows, supporting the life.

The semantic meanings of the above and the similar formations are truly unlimited. However, it is easy to recognize the core Inner Truths and mysteries on a subtle level, once we turn our attention to the inner worlds on the regular basis and work and study diligently, without prejudices or fixed expectations.

On the other side, an initial "one inch mistake" can make one miss the target by a mile and carry the practitioner into the rough or swampy terrains, from where it takes a lot of effort and suffering to return to the narrow path of the accomplishment of the true goals. The "evil" in Taoism doesn't have a metaphysical foundation, it is just something good, stuck to a wrong place. All possible problems are attributed to the *attachments* to Post-Heaven things (that prevent smooth TC transformation around the pivot point or make the spirit "dizzy" and wandering). The suffering is considered to be primarily caused by the "Three Worms":

- "Egoism" of the Spirit (within upper Dan Tian)
- "Greed" of the Qi (in Middle Dan Tian)
- "Debauchery" of the Essence (in Lower Dan Tian)

It is easy to cause a harm to oneself by trying to suppress the Divine Spark that lies within (also called "Inner Child", "Immortal Embryo" or just an innermost ideal of the better self) and investing personal capabilities and gifts towards the growth of externally impressed and fake, but apparently (based on the repetitive suggestive effect of mass-media, environmental influence etc.) socially desirable surrogates[38] (like predatory attitude, attachment to material possessions, social status, hedonism etc.).

However, the *Primordial Origin* or all our actions, the purity and clear slate of a child or the sage (who are both in the contact with Oneness) is always at the reach of the hand. We are in power to spiritually release the externally enforced attachments at any moment, and once this happens (initiating the cycle of change), the Laws of Heaven would gradually take care of the necessary processing in the world.

A complete sincerity towards oneself[39] in decisions and actions is a key to the fulfillment, as any ego constructs or attachments can disrupt the simplicity (any Post-Heaven attachment would naturally cause pain during any TC

---

38) Such illusionary acceptance is usually seen in various combinations of "socially approved" but rigid and blind norms on one side and the "contra-culture" (street desperation) on the other, well symbolized in the Myth of Andromeda where she is chained to the rock (by parents) and in danger of being devoured by the sea beast

39) Even though these two terms are often confused in the modern society and common miss-interpretations of the work of Aleister Crowley, there is an enormous difference between one's *True Free Will* and one's *Voluntarism* or the "Free Whim". While the Ego Wishes are the capricious attachments to the Post-Heaven objects and processes (that cannot be alchemically transformed to the higher states), the Individual True Will or Heavenly Mission is determined by a serious introspection, under full conscience and enhances one's eternal Spirit and the Pre-Heaven Primordial Truth.

transformation of consciousness, as the related physical world *links are not immutable to change*) necessary for the smooth metaphysical transformation. Any deep and sincere aspiration, determined internally as our True Intent, should be achievable, as long as it has been surrendered to the Divine and the causal control in the world of manifestation passed (by Pre-Heaven work e.g. TCs) to the spiritual realm.

Many deep alchemical secrets, some of which are never to be revealed, lie within mentioned, seemingly simple (or far from reality), numerical and allegorical formations. "True People" (Zhen Ren) according to the Taoist view, are not assumed to be sexless, but female and male Immortals, who are eternally resolving the mysteries of Divine Love.

Realization and actualization of the human potentials, described[40] in the present text and other mystical manuscripts is a serious, demanding and life-long task. It requires dedication, sobriety (rigorous re-evaluation from different angles generally prevents slips into fantasy), constancy and the righteousness of an individual. The usual superficial approaches, such as pure curiosity, criticism from a fixed point of view or the intent to use acquired knowledge and power for selfish needs, will automatically disconnect an aspirant from the infinite source of mystery. On the other side, a sincere and dedicated Individual study generally brings results beyond anything imaginable on "this side of the mountain".

No direct lineage or otherwise "proprietary" transmissions (generally passed under oath or "confidentiality agreement" in a restricted cycle) are presented here, as they have the place in the other, private, or teacher-student practical part of study. However, every sincerely recorded holistic work

---

40) The philosophy is similar to the source code of a computer program, it needs to be *compiled,* transformed into the "machine executable code" (the unique physical and emotional setup of the practitioner, along with links to the personal "libraries" of one's knowledge and energy) to be really applicable in practice.

mirrors the reality, so that even this crude translation and commentary attempt, based on publicly available information and some direct experiences in the domain, should provide a basic, but usable theoretical framework for a deeper individual study.

The practice system of "Jade Writing", even though it has the editor's deepest respect, also does not present the only possible methodology to achieve the targeted results, as the same core concept and process can always be expressed and implemented using many languages and self-development paradigms (similarly as the same *design pattern* can work successfully in very different software development frameworks). Also, a rich tree, with many strong branches of the internal or external specialization classes, could grow from the apparently simple mystical concepts, due to their deep, holographic nature.

Even though the modern science usually considers the Inner Teachings too subjective to be taken into account in a modern descriptions of the world, the independent research and discovery of the identical spiritual principles (ethnical and cultural flavors aside), at the different sides of the world, by the practitioners who are completely unaware of each other, actually comprises a very *rigorous scientific process*, with an extensive experimental validation.

Our perception of the World affects the World. All sincere points of view regarding the laws of Nature and ourselves come from different personal systems of reference and present the unique reflections of the single, *silent,* infinite Truth that is continuously written to the very texture of the Universe, for the benefit of All.

It is editor's hope that this Introduction, a brief glance to an Infinite Treasure behind the Gates of Mystery, would contribute to a better modern understanding of the ancient Taoist texts and to the more efficient study of the wisdom and the compassion of the old Masters, the noble Authors of the original Jade Writing, before whom he bows.

JADE WRITING

Section I

Huáng	Tíng	Wài	Jǐng	Jīng
黄	庭	外	景	经
Yellow	Court	External	Scenery	Scripture

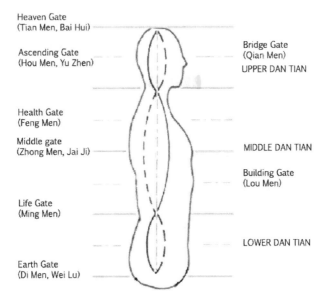

Heaven Gate
(Tian Men, Bai Hui)

Ascending Gate
(Hou Men, Yu Zhen)

Health Gate
(Feng Men)

Middle gate
(Zhong Men, Jai Ji)

Life Gate
(Ming Men)

Earth Gate
(Di Men, Wei Lu)

Bridge Gate
(Qian Men)

UPPER DAN TIAN

MIDDLE DAN TIAN

Building Gate
(Lou Men)

LOWER DAN TIAN

Figure 10: Main gateways on the path of Internal Elixir cultivation

Yellow Court External Scenery Scripture

The External Scenery Scripture, divided into three chapters (for Upper, Middle, and Lower Dan Tian), provides a high-level structural description of the Yellow Court (Individual Field or Body) formation. It defines how our existence is shaped out, polarized into separate systems or sub-totalities, *along the path of the manifestation of Spirit* (as on Figure 3, or the first part of Formula [1]). The detailed life and mission of the elements of the body, along with specific *names* of the spiritual archetypes (their style, magical, or jewel name, or a living function and robe details) and their path of re-integration to Tao is detailed in the Internal Scenery Scripture.

Yellow is the color from the very middle of the light spectrum (symbolizing energy and Earth). The ancient Yellow Court indicates the center of the residential area, the open place in the palace (where residents of the Court meet to privately experience heaven and earth. It connects the chambers of different Ministries of the Court, designated for the life and work of the officials who carry specific functions in the kingdom. The Scripture establishes correspondence between the ancient Emperor Palace, as the center of the kingdom, and the body, as the center of the world (the field of interaction with the environment) of an individual.

The human body and each of its separate organs are mapped to the palaces within the Court. Every actualized, well-formed body function is formed as a unique holographic reflection of the equivalent spiritual archetype from the external hierarchy of the Heavenly Order. Of course, the Individuality itself is the monarch of the own Yellow Court, with a nature and an internal role that is akin to the Jade Emperor. A practitioner works on the integration of the Oneness and Uniqueness, *Cosmos* and *Man*, by accepting and recognizing the mystical designations (from without) and driving (from within) their practical fulfillment in the own, specific circumstances.

上 部 经 第 一
Shàng Bù Jīng Dì Yī
High Section Scripture **No. One**

太 上 闲 居 作 七 言
Tài Shàng Xián Jū Zuò Qī Yán
ancient above idly reside write seven word

解 脱 身 形 及 诸 神。
Jiě Tuō Shēn Xíng Jí Zhū Shén
set free (from) body image and all spirit

上 有 黄 庭 下 关 元
Shàng Yǒu Huáng Tíng Xià Guān Yuán
above there is yellow court below Gate Origin

后 有 幽 阙 前 生 门。
Hòu Yǒu Yōu Què Qián Shēng Mén
behind there is Mystic Watch front Life Gate

呼 吸 庐 间 入 丹 田
Hū Xī Lú Jiān Rù Dān Tián
exhale inhale skull between join Elixir Field

玉 池 清 水 灌 灵 根。
Yù Chí Qīng Shuǐ Guàn Líng Gēn
jade pool clear water irrigate spiritual root

Chapter 1.1

High sovereign, residing in peace, wrote a seven-word scripture,

to tell the secrets how to enhance the individual form and spirit.

Yellow Court[1] is located above, Original Pass[2] is located below.

Quiet Watchtower[3] is behind; Life Gate[4] is at the front.

Let your breath precipitate between three joined Dan Tian,

and clear waters of Jade Pool irrigate Spirit Root.[5]

---

1) Here Yellow Court term indicates an Earth pair of internal organs: in physical body: Spleen and Stomach.

2) CV-4 acupuncture point, 3 inches below the navel, the source of Original (Yuan) Qi.

3) Also Mi Hu or Ming Men, DU-4 between the Kidneys

4) Life Gate here indicates the navel. The metabolism of food and circulation of the life-supporting Qi occurs in abdomen, or the area between Middle and Lower Dan Tian, Ming Men, and Navel points.

5) Jade Pool indicates the source of saliva (and its related internal vitality), under the tongue, Spirit Root indicates the point where Spirit enters manifestation (The Root of Spiritual Being), where the tip of the tongue touches the upper palate (to join Governor and Director, Du and Ren vessel). The "Irrigation of Spirit Root" integrates the assistance of the Upper Dan Tian in regulation of the metabolic functions between the two lower Dan Tians mentioned in 1-4.

Shěn	Néng	Xiū	Zhī	Kě	Cháng	Cún
审	能	修	之	可	长	存。
examine	able	practice	it	can	long	exist

Huáng	Tíng	Zhēn	Rén	Yī	Zhū	Yī
黄	庭	真	人	衣	朱	衣
yellow	court	true	person	clothed	(to) red	clothes

Guān	Yuán	Zhuàng	Yuè	Hé	Liǎng	Mí
关	元	壮	龠	阖	两	靡
gate	origin	luxuriant	shut	door	two	extravagant

Yōu	Què	Xiá	Zhī	Gāo	Wēi	Wēi
幽	阙	侠	之	高	巍	巍
imperial	palace	knight	's	high	lofty	lofty

Dān	Tián	Zhī	Zhōng	Jīng	Qì	Wēi
丹	田	之	中	精	气	微
	Dan Tian	's	middle	Jing	Qi	subtle

Yù	Chí	Qīng	Shuǐ	Shàng	Shēng	Féi
玉	池	清	水	上	生	肥
jade	pool	clear	water	above	produce	fertility

Líng	Gēn	Jiān	Gù	Lǎo	Bù	Shuāi
灵	根	坚	固	老	不	衰。
	Spirit Root		firm	old		no wane

Zhōng	Chí	Yǒu	Shì	Yī	Chì	Yī
中	池	有	士	衣	赤	衣
middle	pool	there is	gentleman	wear	red	clothes

Practice constantly, to achieve longevity.[6]

Yellow Court people wear red clothes.

The radiance of the Original Pass[7] is tightly sealed.

Imperial palace knight comes from the elevated space within space[8].

Essence and Qi in the middle of Dan Tian are profound.

The clear dew from the Jade Pool enables pure potency from above.

Spirit root will be firm, never weakening by time.

In the middle pool, seats a high spirit in red clothes.[9]

---

6) Constantly overcome yourself (Identity Enhancement Symmetry).

7) Previously mentioned Guan Yuan pass should direct energy within (to circulate in Dan Tian), and not allow leaking.

8) Knight indicates the Inner power, Primordial, Yuan Qi (Figure 3). The red color mentioned throughout the text indicates the innermost core role of the spirit/archetype for the specific function, similar to the way blood is crucial for the physical body (Pre-Heaven Qi enables the flow of Post-Heaven Qi that leads the distribution of the body fluids).

9) Indicates Middle Dan Tian – heart area (associated to a Fire element). Its Spirit is Shen – regulating actions from the heart (see Figure 5) of any five-element cycle. Any such cycle is administered by a Heart Spirit, nourished/inspired by the Spirit Root (the place where the tongue bridges Du and Ren vessel), as above.

Héng	Xià	Sān	Cùn	Shén	Suǒ	Jū
横	下	三	寸	神	所	居。
horizontal	below	three	inch	spirit	(to live)	

Zhōng	Wài	Xiāng	Jù	Zhòng	Bì	Zhī
中	外	相	距	重	闭	之
middle	external	mutual	distance	repeatedly	close	it

Shén	Lú	Zhī	Zhōng	Wù	Xiū	Zhì
神	庐	之	中	务	修	治。
spirit	hut	's	middle	shall	repair	manage

Xuán	Yíng	Qì	Guǎn	Shòu	Jīng	Fú
玄	膺	气	管	受	精	符
mystical	receive	Qi	windpipe	receive	essence	charm

Jí	Gù	Zǐ	Jīng	Yǐ	Zì	Chí
急	固	子	精	以	自	持。
urgently	strengthen	son	Essence	to	self-sustain	

Zhái	Zhōng	Yǒu	Shì	Cháng	Yī	Jiàng
宅	中	有	士	常	衣	绛
house	middle	there is	gentleman	always	clothes	red

Zǐ	Néng	Jiàn	Zhī	Kě	Bù	Bìng
子	能	见	之	可	不	病。
if you	can	see	it	can	not ill	

Héng	Lì	Cháng	Chǐ	Yuē	Qí	Shàng
横	立	长	尺	约	其	上
horizontal	stand	long	ruler	about	it's	above

At a horizontal and deep place of the three inches in each direction,[10]

between the center and the circumference of the circle, revolves to keep the residence impregnable.

The center of the spirit residence synchronizes the cultivation.[11]

The mysterious opening of wind channel receives essence of the essence.

Very carefully but resolutely strengthen fresh essence to sustain yourself.

At this seat, there is a high spirit that always wears red clothes.

If you are able to recognize it, you would never get ill.

Around it, a constant proportion is established, channeling the higher reality.

---

10) A pivot mechanism of the Individual Phase Space, that centers specific sets of symmetries. Its manifestation is in the lower Dan Tian area, around the geometrical and gravity center of the body. The rotation of Dan Tian corresponds to a primordial circle "spin" (the basis of the spiral on Figure 4).

11) The joint point of horizontal and vertical lines of TC symmetry works like a hub for the ongoing cultivation of the essence. Spirit that always wears red clothes symbolizes the point of perception that continually goes deeper (red color has the lowest frequency in the visible spectrum), forming a converging series of the synchronization circles in the lower Dan Tian.

Zǐ	Néng	Shǒu	Zhī	Kě	Wú	Yàng
子	能	守	之	可	无	恙。
(ff) you	can	keep	it	can	no	offense

Hū	Xī	Lú	Jiān	Yǐ	Zì	Cháng
呼	吸	庐	间	以	自	偿
inhale	exhale	head	in between	to	self	fulfill

Bǎo	Shǒu	Wán	Jiān	Shēn	Shòu	Qìng
保	守	完	坚	身	受	庆。
protect	keep	intact	strong	body	receive	celebration

Fāng	Cùn	Zhī	Zhōng	Jǐn	Gài	Cáng
方	寸	之	中	谨	盖	藏
square	inch	in between	cautiously	cover	hide	

Jīng	Shén	Huán	Guī	Lǎo	Fù	Zhuàng
精	神	还	归	老	复	壮。
Essence	Spirit	return	back	old	recover	strong

Xiá	Yǐ	Yōu	Jué	Liú	Xià	Jìng
侠	以	幽	厥	流	下	竟
knight	because	quiet	its	flow	down	unexpected

Yǎng	Zǐ	Yù	Shù	Líng	Kě	Zhuàng
养	子	玉	树	令	可	壮
foster	your	jade	tree	cause	can	strong

Zhì	Dào	Bù	Fán	Wú	Páng	Wǔ
至	道	不	烦	无	旁	午
utmost	Tao	no	trouble	no	side	noon

Adjoin it consistently and you will make no errors.

Inhale and exhale from it, to accomplish self-fulfillment,[12]

and guard the whole body firm, capable and ready to receive the experience[13] of wonder.

Carefully hide a square inch in the center as a safe house,

for a spirit to return the old and to to recover fresh and strength.[14]

Remote mysteries flow down to establish completeness.[15]

Foster your Jade Tree[16] in order to extend your abilities.

Great Tao is easy to practice, but you cannot see its highest point.[17]

---

12) Spiritual fruit of the continuous self-centering process.

13) The full mystical experience *creates*, releases energy necessary for both usual body functions and internal alchemy transformations (the type of energy depending on the area of the body that is subject to meditation).

14) Renewed identity goes on, purified.

15) Spiritual Truth (external individual spirit merging within to reside in Dan Tian) and Mystery (the scope of Unknown enveloped by the personal body field) blend together.

16) Jade Tree symbolizes the overall body.

17) Which would be absurd, as it would assume that our seeing capability is above Tao/Divine. The incomprehensible infinity naturally balances the things we can reach.

Líng	Tái	Tōng	Tiān	Lín	Zhōng	Yě
灵	台	通	天	临	中	野
spirit	platform	to	heaven	reach	middle	wildness

Fāng	Cùn	Zhī	Zhōng	Zhì	Guān	Xià
方	寸	之	中	至	关	下
square	inch	in	between	reach	pass	down

Yù	Fáng	Zhī	Zhōng	Zhì	Mén	Hù
玉	房	之	中	至	门	户
jade	room	in	middle	intent	gate	door

Jiē	Shì	Gōng	Zǐ	Jiào	Wǒ	Zhě
皆	是	公	子	教	我	者
all	is	gentleman	son	teach	me	individual

Míng	Táng	Sì	Dá	Fǎ	Hǎi	Yuán
明	堂	四	达	法	海	源
Bright Hall		four	eminent	follow	sea	fountain

Zhēn	Rén	Zǐ	Dān	Dāng	Wǒ	Qián
真	人	子	丹	当	我	前
true	man	son	pellet	manage	my	front

Sān	Guān	Zhī	Zhōng	Jīng	Qì	Shēn
三	关	之	中	精	气	深。
three	pass	's	in between	essence	Qi	deep

Zǐ	Yù	Bù	Sǐ	Xiū	Kūn	Lún
子	欲	不	死	修	昆	仑
Self	want	no	death	build	Kunlun	

The spirit on stage, connected to the Heavens, faces the Unknown in the center.[18]

It descends through a square inch pass of the heavenly gate,

entering a jade room behind the gate.

The True Man residing there is the higher self, a teacher within.

At the top of the upper palate, four clear rivers join the sea of origin.

True Man prepares elixir for the new Self

on a three path junction, where Jing and Qi[19] cross.

If you want this gateway to be impassable for death, build it to be like the Kunlun mountain.

---

18) Stage represents the chosen Mystery of manifestation (e.g. various dualities between spirit and body). An Individual spirit comes to a stage from Heaven (previously achieved Oneness).

19) Physically, the place where Du, Ren and Zhong vessel join in the body, above the upper palate and behind the eyes. In the Phase space, the coordinate center of the intersection of Jing, Qi and Shen or Uniqueness, Oneness and Individuality (see Figure 4).

Yì	Guān	Zhòng	Lóu	Shí	Èr	Jí
绎	官	重	楼	十	二	级
continuous	palace	layer	building	twelve		story

Gōng	Shì	Zhī	Zhōng	Wǔ	Cǎi	Jí
宫	室	之	中	五	采	集
palace	room	's	in middle	five	color	gather

Chì	Shén	Zhī	Zǐ	Zhōng	Chí	Lì
赤	神	之	子	中	池	立
red	spirit 's		son	middle	spa	establish

Xià	Yǒu	Cháng	Chéng	Xuán	Gǔ	Yì
下	有	长	城	玄	谷	邑
below	there is	great	wall	profound	valley	

Cháng	Shēng	Yào	Miào	Fáng	Zhōng	Jí
长	生	要	妙	房	中	急
longevity	need	cautiousness	room	in	middle	hasty

Qì	Juān	Yín	Yù	Zhuān	Zǐ	Jīng
弃	捐	淫	欲	专	子	精。
abandon	lust	desire	focus		your	Essence

Cùn	Tián	Chǐ	Zhái	Kě	Zhì	Shēng
寸	田	尺	宅	可	治	生
inch	land	foot	house	can	manage	life

Xì	Zǐ	Cháng	Liú	Xīn	Ān	Níng
系	子	长	留	心	安	宁。
concern	you	long	keep	heart		peaceful

In a palace made of 12 continuous stores

jade hall in the middle collects the five colors

and red spirit manifests itself in the central pool.[20]

Underneath there is a great wall surrounding a profound valley.[21]

Longevity demands carefulness with the room of desires underneath.[22]

Abandon investing to lust, concentrate on the essence of your essence, Pre-Heaven Jing.

The one-inch entry area within a one-foot land of one's face is so able to govern human life.

Concentration on the formation of one's young self makes possible for the heart to stay always at peace.

---

20) The 12-story pagoda is associated to a throat, Jade Hall to an esophagus, and the middle pool to a heart. A digestion process collects and integrates five elements (flavors or colors) from saliva, the essence of the food.

21) Intestines, where the nutrients are absorbed to body, during the circular passage of the food juice, after its transformation and charging in the stomach.

22) The flow of essence of food to the sexual area, a place where Jing is created, but needs to be preserved for longevity.

推 Tuī	志 Zhì	游 Yóu	神 Shén	三 Sān	奇 Qí	灵 Líng
defer	will	wander	spirit	three	wonder	spirit

闲 Xián	暇 Xiá	无 Wú	事 Shì	心 Xīn	太 Tài	平。Píng
in leisure		no	trouble	heart	peaceful	

常 Cháng	存 Cún	玉 Yù	房 Fáng	神 Shén	明 Míng	达 Dá
often	keep	jade	room	spirit	bright	eminent

时 Shí	念 Niàn	太 Tài	仓 Cāng	不 Bù	饥 Jī	渴 Kě
often	think	Great	Granary	no	hunger	thirst

役 Yì	使 Shǐ	六 Liù	丁 Dīng	玉 Yù	女 Nǚ	谒 Yè
use	service	six	measure	jade	girl	visit

闭 Bì	子 Zǐ	精 Jīng	路 Lù	可 Kě	长 Cháng	活。Huó
close	your	Jing	path	can	long	live

正 Zhèng	室 Shì	之 Zhī	中 Zhōng	神 Shén	所 Suǒ	居 Jū
upright	room	in	middle	spirit	to live	

洗 Xǐ	心 Xīn	自 Zì	治 Zhì	无 Wú	敢 Gǎn	污。Wū
wash	heart	self	cure	no	dare	corrupt

Prevent will[23] from dissipating, but let it join three wonderful spirits.[24]

Let it walk between them, and there would be no problem keeping the heart peaceful and content.

Frequently store the attained bright light to the jade room.

Meditate periodically on the stomach area (Great Granary) to eliminate hunger and thirst.

Once Qi starts flowing, all six Jade Girls[25] will be also present.

Close your essence gate to achieve longevity.

Straighten the room in the middle so spirit would live within.[26]

Cleanse the heart-mind so it would be inclined to self-healing rather than self-intoxicating.

---

23) Zhi, spirit of the Kidneys, or "will-mind", managing the material existence (see Figure 5), shouldn't dissipate through attachments to a material world but should function as a non-reacting catalyst of the alchemical rebirth of Individuality.

24) Body spirits directed upward, towards a higher existence: Hun - spirit of the liver, Shen - spirit of the heart, and Yi - spirit of the spleen reintegrate with the external Primordial Oneness in the jade room.

25) Spirits of Yin (solidifying) energy that correspond to Heavenly stems and Earthly branches with names containing "Ding" (container) character. They protect different aspects, "luck", of one's field or interaction with the world

26) Lower Dan Tian needs to be always pure and fresh for the Primordial Spirit to enter and live within.

| Lì 历 experience | Guān 观 observe | Wǔ 五 five | Zàng 脏 viscera | Shì 视 watch | Jié 节 | Dù 度- tolerance |
| six | mansion | repair | manage | clean | as | plain |

历 观 五 脏 视 节 度-
experience observe five viscera watch tolerance

Liù 六 Fǔ 府 Xiū 修 Zhì 治 Jié 洁 Rú 如 Sù 素。
six mansion repair manage clean as plain

Xū 虚 Wú 无 Zì 自 Rán 然 Dào 道 Zhī 之 Gù 固
void nature self correct Tao 's solid

Wù 物 Yǒu 有 Zì 自 Rán 然 Dào 道 Bù 不 Fán 烦。
substance have self correct Tao no trouble

Chuí 垂 Gǒng 拱 Wú 无 Wéi 为 Shēn 身 Tǐ 体 Ān 安
suspend cup inaction body peaceful

Xū 虚 Wú 无 Zhī 之 Jū 居 Zài 在 Wéi 帏 Jiān 间。
void's residence reside at curtain between

Jì 寂 Mò 寞 Kuàng 旷 Rán 然 Kǒu 口 Bù 不 Yán 言
loneliness upright mouth no say

Xiū 修 Hé 和 Dú 独 Lì 立 Zhēn 真 Rén 人 Guān 官
cultivate harmony independence true man gate

70

Observe five solid organs, to learn their mutual interaction and rhythm.

Six offices manage repair and cleanliness, so they are like white silk.

Void is the nature of the strength of Tao.

Substantial is the nature of the sobriety of Tao.

Non-action with a firm resolution makes the body relaxed and the mind concentrated.[27]

Find the void behind the curtain of the residences of bright spirit.[28]

Do not interact and talk without need, so your city wall is upright and Qi doesn't leak,

however maintain independence and harmony with the world at the same time, in a stance of a True Man.[29]

---

27) Wu Wei, a moment in the time cycle when the extreme stillness is established and we can just let Heaven take its course around our central harmony.

28) A curtain between the two cycles of manifestation, separating Truth and Mystery. The Light of Truth continually penetrates the Mystery, but every Understanding also opens the new space of the Unknown, in the interplay of the light and dark side of Tai Ji (Yin/Yang) flow.

29) Self-sustained and not attached to Post-Heaven manifestations, but continuously helping the world.

Tián	Dàn	Wú	Yù	Yóu	Dé	Yuán
恬	淡	无	欲	游	德	园。
tranquil	no	desire	tour	virtue	park	

Qīng	Jìng	Xiāng	Jié	Yù	Nǚ	Qián
清	净	香	洁	玉	女	前
clear	clean	fragrant	pure	jade	girl	before

Xiū	Dé	Míng	Dá	Shén	Zhī	Mén
修	德	明	达	神	之	门。
cultivate	virtue	bright	eminent	spirit	's	gate

Achieve inner peace and accomplish external things without effort, enjoying the Garden of Virtue.[30]

Clear and fragrant the passage before the entry of the Jade Girl.[31]

Cultivate virtue to avoid distractions in your Primordial spirit manifestation.[32]

---

30) As mentioned in the Introduction, the Inner Peace and the External Prosperity (accomplished by recognizing and directing a continuous process of creation and transformation) have a common root in the Individual Virtue.

31) Open to a spiritual energy action (either for the individual mission in the world or for the internal Qi flow), the process of continuous cultivation, that can be associated with the infinite Mercy of the Primordial (Jade) integration, also symbolized by the goddess Kwan Yin (the Bodhisattva concept) in Buddhism or the personal Kundalini (or Shakti) aspect in Yoga.

32) Primordial, radiant (Yang) Self that is continually renewed, the Buddha ideal or the Individual Shiva aspect in Yoga.

中部经第二
Zhōng Bù Jīng Dì Èr
Middle Section scripture No. Two

作 道 优 游 深 独 居
Zuò Dào Yōu Yóu Shēn Dú Jū
practice Tao high wander deep alone live

扶 养 性 命 守 虚 无。
Fú Yǎng Xìng Mìng Shǒu Xū Wú
support raise life essence living keep void not

恬 淡 无 为 何 思 虑
Tián Dàn Wú Wéi Hé Sī Lǜ
tranquil mild non doing why think concern

羽 翼 已 成 正 扶 疏
Yǔ Yì Yǐ Chéng Zhèng Fú Shū
feature wing already grown luxuriant well-spaced

长 生 久 视 乃 飞 去
Cháng Shēng Jiǔ Shì Nǎi Fēi Qù
always grow long look therefore fly overcome

五 行 参 差 同 根 蒂
Wǔ Xíng Cān Chā Tóng Gēn Dì
five forms take part uneven common root stem

三 五 合 气 要 本 一
Sān Wǔ Hé Qì Yào Běn Yī
three five join Qi require original one

Chapter 1.2

Practitioners of the Tao should be detached and self-sustained.

Nurture the essential nature and life and guard the void.

Tranquility brings inner happiness and clear worries,

helping to achieve the lightness potential, an ability to float over the obstacles or to dissolve them

Always prosperous, deep understanding will finally overcome everything.

The five transformations have different forms but a common base,

each ruling during one of the five phases of the Qi flow, that oscillates between the two extremes, centered around the middle[1] void.

---

1) Various natural cycles in the body and the Universe can be represented (in the phase space, or spiritual reality) by periodic functions of arbitrary complexity and shape, which are, however, always based on the series of simple functions (as the periodic Natural phenomena can be represented by Fourier transformation) that can be defined by its five gradients ("intents") and three gradient reversal points (as on Figure 5).

Shuí	Yǔ	Gòng	Zhī	Dǒu	Rì	Yuè
谁	与	共	之	斗	日	月
who	with	altogether	it	star	Sun	Moon

Bào	Yù	Huái	Zhū	Hé	Zī	Shì
抱	玉	怀	珠	和	子	室
hold	jade	think	jewel	together	self	room

Zǐ	Néng	Shǒu	Yī	Wàn	Shì	Bì
子	能	守	一	万	事	毕
child	can	keep	one	10000	matter	finish

Zǐ	Zì	Yǒu	Zhī	Chí	Wù	Shī
子	自	有	之	持	勿	失
child	self	have	it	hold	no	lose

Jí	Dé	Bù	Sǐ	Rù	Jīn	Shì
即	得	不	死	入	金	室
to	gain	no	death	enter	gold	room

Chū	Rì	Rù	Yuè	Shì	Wú	Dào
出	日	入	月	是	吾	道
out	sun	enter	moon	is	my	Tao

Tiān	Qī	Dì	Sān	Huí	Xiāng	Shǒu
天	七	地	三	回	相	守
heaven	seven	earth	three	round	mutually	adjoin

Shēng	Jiàng	Jìn	Tuì	Hé	Nǎi	Jiǔ
升	降	进	退	合	乃	久。
ascend	descend	advance	withdraw	gather	so	long-lasting

Each operation has Sun, Moon, and Star aspects joined.[2]

Hold the jade, think the pearl, to complete the room for the inner child.

You can then fully complete one or 10,000 things.

When you discover your own existence, hold it and do not lose it.

Desiring to eliminate death, enter the gold room.[3]

Exhale far out with the Sun, inhale deep in with the Moon; this is the Individual Tao.[4]

The seven cycles of Heaven and three cycles of Earth mutually support each other.[5]

Ascend and descend, advance and withdraw, diligently gathering what is between.

---

2) Balance and integration of the Three Treasures: Jing (Uniqueness, star, Man), Qi (Oneness, Moon, Earth), and Shen (Individuality, Sun, Heaven)

3) Close the gate of Death (Yin), open the Gate of Life (Yang, symbolized by gold; a metal element in general signifies the first phase of rebuilding oneself), the Ming Men pass.

4) Moon is an internal void formation, an ability of accepting a Divine Spirit and its gifts from without (as described in the Introduction), Sun is the internal light, awakened by enlightenment, that leads our action of loving the Divine back. Both factors hide in every aspect of the Individual Universe.

5) Seven stars give light to the three treasures through five phases, in the process of the formation of unique existence (Heaven to Earth flow). The inner awakening (light within), based on the transformation of the three treasures, occurs along the return path (Earth to Heaven, or 1-3-5-7-9, on Figure 6) to Oneness.

Yù	Shí	Luò	Luò	Shì	Wú	Bǎo
玉	石	落	落	是	吾	宝
jade	stone	clear	looking	is	my	treasure

Zǐ	Zì	Yǒu	Zhī	Hé	Bù	Shǒu
子	自	有	之	何	不	守
child	self	possess	it	why	not	keep

Xīn	Xiǎo	Gēn	Jī	Yǎng	Huá	Cǎi
心	晓	根	基	养	华	彩
Heart	know	root	foundation	nurture	magnificent	variety

Fú	Tiān	Shùn	Dì	Hé	Cáng	Jīng
服	天	顺	地	合	藏	精。
obey	heaven	obey	earth	altogether	hide	essence

Qī	Rì	Zhī	Wǔ	Huí	Xiāng	Huì
七	日	之	五	回	相	会
seven	day	's	five	round	mutually	meet

Kūn	Lún	Zhī	Shàng	Bù	Mí	Wù
昆	仑	之	上	不	迷	误
Kunlun Mtn.		's	top	no	lost	delay

Jiǔ	Yuán	Zhī	Shān	Hé	Tíng	Tíng
九	原	之	山	何	亭	亭
mine	origin	's	mountain	how	upright	

Zhōng	Yǒu	Zhēn	Rén	Kě	Shǐ	Líng
中	有	真	人	可	使	令
in between	there is	true	man	can	make	order

A jade stone, clear and graceful, is a personal treasure.[6]

It is the One thing physically generated by oneself, so why not keep it?

When mind has a foundation, it can generate a magnificent variety.

Serve Heaven, respect Earth, store the essence where they join.

The five phases of seven stars mutually engage.

The top of Kunlun mountain knows no confusion.

The Nine Origins of the Mountain merge with Heaven.[7]

Between them, there is a True Man who can make order.

---

6) Jing stored in lower Dan Tian, the seed of personal rebirth.

7) Nine peaks delineated at the ring around the top of the head, (see Figure 8 and 11) indicating a connection with the nine-fold aspects of change (or transitions of time), as described in the Introduction.

蔽 Bì shelter	以 Yǐ with	紫 Zǐ purple	宫 Gōng palace	丹 Dān elixir	城 Chéng wall	楼 Lóu tower
侠 Xiá knight	以 Yǐ with	日 Rì sun	月 Yuè moon	如 Rú seem	明 Míng bright	珠 Zhū jewel
万 Wàn 10,000	岁 Suì age	照 Zhào	照 Zhào shine	非 Fēi not	有 Yǒu have	期 Qī term
外 Wài external	本 Běn origin	三 Sān three	阳 Yáng Yang	物 Wù matter	自 Zì self	来 Lái come
内 Nèi internal	养 Yǎng restrain	三 Sān three	神 Shén spirit	可 Kě can	长 Cháng long	生 Shēng live
魂 Hún soul	欲 Yù want	上 Shàng ascend	天 Tiān heaven	魄 Pò spirit	入 Rù enter	渊 Yuān abyss
还 Huán return	魂 Hún soul	返 Fǎn return	魄 Pò soul	道 Dào Tao	自 Zì self	然。Rán natural
璇 Xuán jade	玑 Jī pearl	结 Jié solidify	珠 Zhū refine	环 Huán circle	无 Wú no	端 Duān end

80

He sits in a shelter in a purple office above the wall tower.

The knight of Sun and Moon, he looks like a bright jewel.

He is constantly cultivating for tens of thousands years, without break.

Taking three Yang lights from without to nurture the three treasures within.[8]

Internally cultivated three spirits can enhance one's life.

Earthly spirit wants to ascend to Heaven, Heavenly spirit wants to enter the abyss.[9]

Integration of these Earthly and Heavenly spirits to Tao makes one perfect[10].

Thus formed, Jade pearl is refined[11] and solidified in the spiral transformation circles without end.

---

8) Intake the lights of the Star, Moon and Sun of the three levels of brightness to cultivate own Spiritual light, residing in silence.

9) Hun, spirit of Wood (Liver), tends to ascend. Po, spirit of Metal (Lungs), tends to descend (see Figure 5 for their gradients). Their intents are comparable to the archetypes presented in Tarot cards Magus (levitating above or commanding over the elements) and Fool (about to enter the abyss). Even though the descending gradient of Po can be an obstacle at specific times (e.g. in persisting attachment to the material), it is a part of the natural cycle to dive into new challenges to resolve them.

10) Perseverance in the center of the cycles, not subjecting Individuality to either the descending (Oneness to Uniqueness) or the ascending phase (Uniqueness to Oneness) of subordinate spirits.

11) In a continuous cultivation, only the achieved perfection could be really perfected further.

Yù	Pìn	Jīn	Yuè	Shēn	Wán	Jiān
玉	牝	金	钥	身	完	坚。
jade	girl	gold	key	body	intact	strong

Zài	Dì	Xuán	Tiān	Zhōu	Qián	Kūn
载	地	悬	天	周	乾	坤
carry	earth	suspend	heaven	entire	heaven	earth

Xiàng	Yǐ	Sì	Shí	Chì	Rú	Dān
象	以	四	时	赤	如	丹
appearance	four	season	red	as if	elixir

Qián	Yǎng	Hòu	Bēi	Liè	Qí	Mén
前	仰	后	卑	列	其	门
front	upward	back	humble	arrange	its	gate

Xuǎn	Yǐ	Huán	Dān	Yǔ	Xuán	Quán
选	以	还	丹	与	玄	泉
select	as to	choose	pellet	and	Mystical	Pond

Xiàng	Guī	Yǐn	Qì	Zhì	Líng	Gēn
象	龟	引	气	致	灵	根
elephant	tortoise	lead	Qi	reach	spirit	root

Zhōng	Yǒu	Zhēn	Rén	Jīn	Jīn	Jīn
中	有	真	人	巾	金	巾。
in between	there is	true	man	clothes	gold	clothes

Fù	Jiǎ	Chí	Fú	Kāi	Qī	Mén
负	甲	持	符	开	七	门
carry	armor	hold	magic	open	seven	gate

Gold Yang in Jade Yin unlocks a vibrant health of the body.

Carry on engagement with matter, while staying connected to spirit, to accomplish integration of Heaven and Earth.

Feel like you are always one with Heaven, walking the Eight Ba Gua[12] circle.

Four seasons would appear clear as the parts of the elixir.

Noble front, modest back are in balance at the sides of the central gate.[13]

Select a combination of the desired elixir ingredients and generate it in a mystical pond.[14]

Elephant tortoise leads Qi to reach the Spirit Root.[15]

In between, there is a True Man wearing gold clothes,[16]

in armor, possessing magical gestures to open the seven gates.[17]

---

12) Through Three Dan Tian, we are connected to the Heaven (Tao); walking along (temporal aspects) the path of change, Eight Ba Gua, between South and North on Earth, we engage the world.

13) Qian is a trigram of the front, south, symbolizing creativity; Kun is trigram of back, north, symbolizing receptivity, understanding.

14) Kidneys correspond to North, Water, and a source of the elixir.

15) The tortoise is symbol of the North, Water, and all "Yi Jing" trigrams. A tortoise swallowing breath alchemically corresponds to the ingestion of Pre-Heaven Qi, to merge with Post-Heaven Qi.

16) The overall integration (pivot) point of Individuality.

17) Gates through which elixir has to pass are shown in Figure 10.

Cǐ	Fēi	Zhī	Yè	Shí	Shì	Gēn
此	非	枝	叶	实	是	根
this	not	branch	leaves	actually	is	root

Zhòu	Yè	Sī	Zhī	Kě	Cháng	Cún
昼	夜	思	之	可	长	存
day	night	think	it	can	long	live

Xiān	Rén	Zào	Shì	Fēi	Yǒu	Yì
仙	人	造	士	非	有	异
immortal man		educated man		not	possess	difference

Jī	Jìng	Suǒ	Zhì	Hé	Zhuān	Rén
积	精	所	致	和	专	仁
accumulate Jing		cause	reach	focus	kindness,	

Rén	Jiē	Shí	Gū	Yǔ	Wǔ	Wèi
人	皆	食	谷	与	五	味
man	all	eat	grain	and	five	flavor

Dú	Shí	Tài	Hé	Yīn	Yáng	Qì
独	食	太	和	阴	阳	气
sngle	eat	Great	Harmony	Yin Yang		Qi

Gù	Néng	Bù	Sǐ	Tiān	Xiāng	Jì
故	能	不	死	天	相	既。
therefore	can	not	die	heaven	with both.	

Shì	Shuo	Wǔ	Zàng	Gè	Yǒu	Fāng
试	说	五	脏	各	有	方
try	say	five	viscera	each	have	direction

84

He doesn't put emphasis on leaves but to the root of the existence.

Once all gates are opened and the elixir settles, you need to meditate day and night[18] to obtain longevity.

Immortal man and educated man are both cultivated and not different in principle.[19]

Accumulate Essence (Jing) with devotion and focus on kindness to all.

Ordinary men eat Post-Heaven grains of Earth and enjoy Five Flavors.

Self-sustained men ingest Yin and Yang Qi[20] from the Great Harmony of Heaven,

So they cannot die, as there is a Pre-Heaven essence within.

Each of five viscera has its own direction.[21]

---

18) Blending Yin and Yang phase of the day and void and light of the personal existence, into the Tao.

19) Man educated in Taoism can visualize the alchemical steps on the mental plane and externally, reflecting morality and wisdom, like a Moon. Tao Immortal, through diligent and dedicated practice, became able to manifest the same principal patterns in his own body and good deeds in the world, like a Sun.

20) The recombination of the Pre-Heaven polarities (in the Highest Purity) into a three-fold foundation of existence (where they are reflected, along with the Primordial unity) is the only unlimited source for a continual cycle of life.

21) Ascending, ruling, descending, and keeping the root (see Figure 5 in the Introduction).

Xīn	Wéi	Guó	Zhǔ	Wǔ	Zàng	Wáng
心	为	国	主	五	脏	王
Heart	is	country	master	five	viscera	king

Shòu	Yì	Dòng	Jìng	Qì	Dé	Xíng
受	意	动	静	气	得	行
receive	will	movement	silence	Qi	then	move

Dào	Zì	Jiāng	Wǒ	Shén	Míng	Guāng
道	自	将	我	神	明	光
Tao	self	support	me	spirit	bright	shine

Zhòu	Rì	Zhào	Zhào	Yè	Zì	Shǒu
昼	日	照	照	夜	自	守
daytime	Sun	shine	shine	nighttime	self	observe

Kě	Zì	Dé	Yǐn	Jī	Zì	Bǎo
渴	自	得	饮	饥	自	饱。
thirst	naturally	obtain	liquid	hunger	self	satisfy.

Jīng	Lì	Liù	Fǔ	Cáng	Mǎo	Yǒu
经	历	六	府	藏	卯	酉
experience		six	mansion	hide	Mao	You

Tōng	Wǒ	Jīng	Huá	Diào	Yīn	Yáng
通	我	精	华	调	阴	阳
understand	my	essence		harmonize		Yin Yang

Zhuǎn	Yáng	Zhī	Yīn	Cáng	Yú	Jiǔ
转	阳	之	阴	藏	于	九
turn	Yang	's	Yin	hide		at nine

Heart is the country master and the king of five viscera.

It accepts the silent intent of Qi to move,[22]

obtains support from a spirit presence to develop the light,

shining brightly at daytime and self-observing at nighttime.

Thus it can satisfy its own hunger and thirst.

It collects the Yin in a six-fold cycle between the Earthly branches of Mao and You.[23]

Understands the own Nature and adjusts Yin and Yang transformation.

Activates the Yang Creation, while hiding Yin, through the nine cycles.[24]

---

22) Silence indicates a gradient that neither descends nor ascends, (above and below extreme of the function on Figure 5).

23) 4th (Rabbit) and 10th (Rooster) earthly branch correspond to evening and morning, or the central back and the front point of the body. Heart also physically collect impure (Yin) blood through the veins and pushes out pure (Yang) blood through the arteries.

24) Nine is the number of Heaven and Six number of Earth (see the commentary of Figure 9), their interaction defines various levels of Life.

常 能 行 之 可 不 老。
Cháng Néng Xíng Zhī Kě Bù Lǎo
often can practice it able not old

肝 之 为 气 修 而 长
Gān Zhī Wéi Qì Xiū Ér Cháng
Liver is serve Qi slender and eternal

罗 列 五 脏 主 三 光
Luó Liè Wǔ Zàng Zhǔ Sān Guāng
set out five viscera in charge three light

上 合 三 焦 下 玉 浆
Shàng Hé Sān Jiāo Xià Yù Jiāng
above join Triple Burner below Jade Paste

我 神 魂 魄 在 中 央
Wǒ Shén Hún Pò Zài Zhōng Yāng
my spirits Heart Liver Lung Kidney middle center

精 液 流 泉 去 鼻 香
Jīng Yè Liú Quán Qù Bí Xiāng
essence liquid flow spring go nose aroma

立 于 玄 膺 含 明 堂
Lì Yú Xuán Yīng Hán Míng Táng
stand at Mysterious Well connect Bright Hall

Practice often to control aging.

Liver Qi is restorative and constant.[25]

It orders the five viscera and is in charge of the three lights.[26]

Above it joins the Triple Burner, below it produces a Jade Juice.[27]

Individuality spirit is in the middle.

Jing liquid flows above to integrate with Qi inhaled through the nose.

Establish the Mysterious Well connectivity to the Hall of Light.[28]

---

25) Always sustains a new life, according the nature of the Wood element.

26) It is a base of the three ascending body spirits: Hun (Liver, Wood), Shen (Heart, Fire), and Yi (Spleen, Earth).

27) Bile that dissolves the fat and helps the utilization of the body energy.

28) The saliva path, from the point where tongue touches the upper palate down to the Stomach and Liver. The Hall of Light center, above the point where tongue touches the upper palate (joining Du vessel descending from GV 23, Ming Tang and Ren vessel at front) regulates an integration of the raising Kong Qi (coming with an air from the nose) and Zhong Qi (that comes in food and the generated saliva).

通 我 华 精 调 阴 阳。
Tōng Wǒ Huá Jīng Diào Yīn Yáng
understand my essence harmonize Yin Yang

雷 电 霹 雳 往 相 闻
Léi Diàn Pī Lì Wǎng Xiāng Wén
thunder electric thunder lightning to mutually hear

右 酉 左 卯 是 吾 室。
Yòu Yǒu Zuǒ Mǎo Shì Wú Shì
right You left Mao is my room

90

Understand your own essence and harmonize Yin and Yang.

Like thunder and lighting, the two Qi are mystically bound.

Between the You point on the right and Mao point on the left support the rebirth of Individuality.[29]

---

29) East or Morning (Mao) and West or Evening (You) reflecting the opening and closing of the circle of time, are two parts of symmetry integrated in identity and providing the growth of the Individuality in the center.

下 部 经 第 三
Xià Bù Jīng Dì Sān

Below Section scripture   **No. Three**

伏 Fú	于 Yú	志 Zhì	门 Mén	候 Hòu	天 Tiān	道 Dào
surrender	at	will	gate	wait	heaven	Tao

近 Jìn	在 Zài	子 Zǐ	身 Shēn	还 Huán	自 Zì	守 Shǒu
close	at	master	oneself	yet	self	observe

清 Qīng	静 Jìng	无 Wú	为 Wéi	神 Shén	留 Liú	止 Zhǐ
pure	calm	inaction		spirit	remain	still

精 Jīng	神 Shén	上 Shàng	下 Xià	开 Kāi	分 Fēn	理。 Lǐ
essence	spirit	above	below	open	divide	(put in order)

精 Jīng	候 Hòu	天 Tiān	道 Dào	长 Cháng	生 Shēng	草 Cǎo
patiently	await	heaven	Tao	long	life	grass

七 Qī	窍 Qiào	已 Yǐ	通 Tōng	不 Bù	知 Zhī	老。 Lǎo
seven	aperture	upon	connect	not	know	old

还 Huán	坐 Zuò	天 Tiān	门 Mén	侯 Hóu	阴 Yīn	阳 Yáng
still	sit	heaven	gate	wait	Yin Yang	

Chapter 1.3

Surrender at the Gate of Will waiting for Heavenly Tao.

Even those who have gone far in the self-mastery, should always continue introspection.

In pure and calm non-action spirit remains still[1].

Above is the vitality of integrated essence and spirit, world below opens into the orders of two[2].

Patiently await heavenly Tao[3] constantly cultivating the growth of the plant in the silence.

After connection of seven gates[4] you will not know aging.

Sit still at the heavenly gate[5] waiting for the noble Yin and Yang to emerge.

---

1) Wu Wei, action without action, also period of time around noon

2) Symmetries (Yin and Yang) integrate to Asymmetrical (Tao) Transcendence, that again breaks into new pair of Symmetries

3) This relates to an upward flow of the Heavenly River (see Figure 11). In one Chinese proverb it is mentioned that "difficulties look overwhelming on the way of righteousness, but when the great Tao shines, they turn to benefits",

4) Seven gates (listed in Comment 17 of Chapter 1.2) lie on Microcosmic Orbit of Du and Ren vessel, and their connection means the opening of the Microcosmic Orbit for the continuous Qi flow.

5) Wait for a new (Yin Yang) mystery at the gate of Heavenly Peace (Ming Tang) and for a (Tao) Truth at the Gate of Will (Dan Tian).

Xià	Yú	Hóu	Lóng	Shén	Míng	Tōng
下	于	喉	咙	神	明	通。
below	of	larynx	throat	spirit	understand	communicate

Guò	Huá	Gài	Xià	Qīng	Qiě	Liáng
过	华	盖	下	清	且	凉
cross	canopy	underneath		refresh	and	cool

Rù	Qīng	Líng	Yuān	Jiàn	Wú	Xíng
入	清	灵	渊	见	吾	形
enter	clear	sprit	abyss	see	my	image

Qī	Chéng	Huán	Dān	Kě	Cháng	Shēng
期	成	还	丹	可	长	生。
term	fulfilled	return	elixir	can	extend	life

Huán	Guò	Huá	Chí	Dòng	Shèn	Jīng
还	过	华	池	动	肾	精。
still	over	splendid	pool	move	kidney	essence

Lì	Yú	Míng	Táng	Wàng	Dān	Tián
立	于	明	堂	望	丹	田
stand	at	Light Hall		look over	Dan Tian	

Jiāng	Shǐ	Zhū	Shén	Kāi	Mìng	Mén
将	使	诸	神	开	命	门
command	employ	all	spirit	open	Life	Gate

Tōng	Lì	Tiān	Dào	Cún	Líng	Gēn
通	利	天	道	存	灵	根
connect	benefit	heaven	Tao	exist	Spirit Root	

Jade Liquid flows down the throat to be intercepted by a spirit of the communication,

refreshing and cooling the splendid canopy underneath[6].

In a large and clear spirit pool one can see the own image.

At the point of the completed circulation, you are extending your life.

Still over splendid pool circulate your Kidneys' essence,

standing at Ming Tang[7] look over Dan Tian.

command to all subordinate spirits to open the Life Gate[8].

Connect goodness of the Heavenly Tao to the reality of the Spirit Root.

---

6) Lungs are invigorated by a descending spirit of vitality.

7) Ming Tang or "Hall of Brightness", center of consciousness, the point on upper palate, residing directly under Shang Xing ("Upper Star") point. It presides over the function (Ren) vessel.

8) Ming Men (GV-4), a point of origin of the personally generated energy that, once awaken, rises through the governor (Du) vessel.

Yīn	Yáng	Liè	Bù	Ruò	Liú	Xīng
阴	阳	列	布	若	流	星。
Yin Yang	arrange	disseminate		seem	flow	star

Gān	Qì	Zhōu	Huán	Zhōng	Wú	Duān
肝	气	周	还	终	无	端
Liver	energy	all over	circulate	eventually	no ending	

Fèi	Zhī	Wéi	Qì	Sān	Jiāo	Qǐ
肺	之	为	气	三	焦	起
Lung	act	as	energy	Triple Heater		start

Shàng	Fú	Tiān	Mén	Hóu	Gù	Dào
上	伏	天	门	侯	故	道
above	seat	heaven	gate	rests	ancient	Tao

Jīn	Yè	Lǐ	Quán	Tōng	Liù	Fǔ
津	液	醴	泉	通	六	府
saliva	fluid	sweet	wine	spring	six	mansion

Suí	Bí	Shàng	Xià	Kāi	Liǎng	Ěr
随	鼻	上	下	开	两	耳
along	nose	above	below	open	two	ear

Kuī	Shì	Tiān	Dì	Cún	Tóng	Zǐ
窥	视	天	地	存	童	子
	peek	heaven	earth	keep	virgin	child

Diào	Hé	Jīng	Huá	Zhì	Fà	Chǐ
调	和	精	华	治	发	齿
conciliate		essence	splendid	cure	hair	tooth

Yin and Yang arrangements would disseminate like a path of stars.

Qi from Liver circulates all over, without ending.

Lung works to set out flow of energy generated by Triple Burner.

Above the seat of Heavenly Gate rests an Ancient Tao.

Sweet wine of saliva fluid connects Six Mansions[9]

Matching the opening to the world above, through the bridge of the nose, two ears open to receive the world below

Observe all from heaven and earth[10] to generate virgin new self-existence[11].

Complete transformation of splendid essence to regenerate teeth and hair.

---

9) Fu (bowel) organs

10) External heaven and earth also correspond to top and bottom of the body.

11) "Immortal Fetus" of the renewed Individual, built at the pivot point of symmetries (material world from below) and asymmetry (spirit world from above).

Yán	Sè	Rùn	Zé	Bù	Fù	Bái
颜	色	润	泽	不	复	白
colorful	smooth	luster		not	return	white

Xià	Yú	Hóu	Lóng	Hé	Luò	Luò
下	于	喉	咙	何	落	落
descend	to	larynx	throat	which	receives	

Zhū	Shén	Jiē	Huì	Xiāng	Qiú	Suǒ
诸	神	皆	会	相	求	索
all	spirit	meat	each other		seeking	arrangement

Xià	Dà	Jiàng	Gōng	Zǐ	Huá	Sè
下	大	绛	宫	紫	华	色
below	big	crimson	palace	purple	splendid	color

Yǐn	Cáng	Huá	Gài	Guān	Tōng	Lú
隐	藏	华	盖	观	通	庐
secret	harbor	magnificent	canopy	watch	entire	cottage

Zhuān	Shǒu	Xīn	Shén	Zhuān	Xiāng	Hū
专	守	心	神	转	相	呼
devoted	guard	heart	spirit	turn	mutually	cry out

Guān	Wǒ	Shén	Míng	Bì	Zhū	Xié
观	我	神	明	辟	诸	邪
watch	my	spirit	wisdom	ward off	all	evil

Pí	Shén	Huán	Guī	Yī	Dà	Jiā
脾	神	还	归	依	大	家
Spleen	spirit	return		depend on	everybody	

98

Hair color will shine and it will not turn white.

Descend the introspection down the throat where liquid drops down,

All spirits unite with each other in sequence.

Below the large Crimson Palace, gather the splendid purple color.[12]

Harbor Splendid Canopy watching the entire cottage[13].

Devotedly supervise Heart Spirit while releasing the Ego image of oneself.

Watch how the Wisdom Spirit of Individuality shakes off all the evil.

Spleen (Intent) Spirit also returns to oneness after the mission of all other spirits is complete.

---

12) The Spirit (purple) condenses down from the Middle Dan Tian (Crimson Palace) to the center of the body (Lower Dan Tian).

13) Spleen (element Earth), that completes one cycle of the Totality Centering process, stimulates Lungs (Splendid Canopy) that are initiating a new transformation cycle.

Zhì	Yú	Wèi	Guǎn	Tōng	Xū	Wú
致	于	胃	管	通	虚	无
extend	at	stomach	pipe	connect	nihility	

Cáng	Yǎng	Líng	Gēn	Bù	Fù	Kū
藏	养	灵	根	不	复	枯
collect	foster	Spirit	Root	not	again	wither

Bì	Sāi	Mìng	Mén	Rú	Yù	Dū
闭	塞	命	门	如	玉	都
close	up	life	gate	seem	jade	capital

Shòu	Chuán	Wàn	Suì	Jiāng	Yǒu	Yú
寿	传	万	岁	将	有	余
longevity	pass	10,000	age	will	have	surplus

Pí	Zhōng	Zhī	Shén	Zhǔ	Zhōng	Gōng
脾	中	之	神	主	中	宫
Spleen	(in the middle of)		spirit	manage	Middle	Palace

Zhāo	Huì	Wǔ	Zàng	Liè	Sān	Guāng
朝	会	五	脏	列	三	光
pilgrimage	to	five	viscera	arrange	three	light

Shàng	Hé	Tiān	Mén	Hé	Míng	Táng
上	合	天	门	合	明	堂
above	joint	heaven	gate	joint	Light	Hall

Tōng	Lì	Liù	Fǔ	Diào	Wǔ	Xíng
通	利	六	府	调	五	行
connect	benefit	six	mansion	adjust	five	forms

Extend introspection to the stomach hall to connect to the void.

Preserve and foster Spirit Root, not to ever wither.

Close the Life Gate to the Jade Capital

A new cycle comes from the existence of ten thousand years.

Spleen spirit in the middle manages the Central Office.

Its pilgrimage along five viscera arranges the three lights[14].

Above, it joins Heavenly Gate through Hall of Brightness,

connecting benefits of the six mansions to the five forms[15].

---

14) A standing wave of the new Qi is formed within Three Burners (upper, medium and low) in the central body area.

15) Six bowel (Fu) organs, transporting fluids to be stored in five solid (Zang) organs are all regulated by the Spirit that enters the Upper Dan Tian.

Jīn	Mù	Shuǐ	Huǒ	Tǔ	Wéi	Wáng
金	木	水	火	土	为	王
gold	wood	water	fire	earth	is	king

Tōng	Lì	Xuè	Mài	Hàn	Wéi	Jiāng
通	利	血	脉	汗	为	浆
connect	benefit	blood	pulse	sweat	is	paste

Xiū	Hù	Qī	Qiào	Qù	Bù	Xiáng
修	护	七	窍	去	不	祥
repair	protect	seven	aperture	rid	not auspicious	

Rì	Yuè	Liè	Bù	Zhāng	Yīn	Yáng
日	月	列	布	张	阴	阳
Sun	Moon	arrange	display	expand	Yin Yang	

Èr	Shén	Xiāng	Dé	Huà	Yù	Yīng
二	神	相	得	化	玉	英
two	spirit	mutually	gain	transform	Jade Bravery	

Shàng	Bǐng	Yuán	Qì	Mìng	Yì	Cháng
上	禀	元	气	命	益	长
above	endow	primordial	energy	life	increase	length

Wǔ	Zàng	Zhī	Zhǔ	Shèn	Zuì	Jīng
五	脏	之	主	肾	最	精
five	viscera 's	master	kidney	most	essential	

Fú	Yú	Tài	Yīn	Chéng	Wú	Xíng
伏	于	太	阴	成	吾	形
surrender	to	ancient	Yin	form	my	image

Between metal, water, wood and fire, earth is the King[16].

Connects benefits of heart pulses and lung sweat to the own healing serum.

Repairs and protects seven aperture and eliminates everything that is not auspicious.

Sun and Moon arrangement reflects in the internal Yin and Yang development.

Two spirits cooperate to transform Jade Bravery[17].

From the above, heavenly energy granted to the Individual nourishes the life.

Between five viscera, Kidneys are most essential.

Surrender concept of oneself to ancient Yin to reestablish own image.

---

16) Even though heart spirit performs the highest function in a specific cycle, spleen spirit integrates the old and the new cycle.

17) An individual's ability to make the breakthroughs along the Path, between the pairs of polarities of the cultivation.

出 Chū out	入 Rù in	二 Èr two	窍 Qiào aperture	合 Hé join	黄 Huáng yellow	庭 Tíng court
呼 Hū exhale	吸 Xī inhale	虚 Xū	无 Wú nihility	见 Jiàn see	吾 Wú my	形 Xíng image
强 Qiáng Strengthen	我 Wǒ my	筋 Jīn tendon	骨 Gǔ bone	血 Xuè blood	脉 Mài artery	盛 Shèng flourishing
恍 Huǎng	惚 Hū (as if in a dream)	不 Bù not	见 Jiàn see	过 Guò cross	清 Qīng clear	灵 Líng spirit
坐 Zuò sit	于 Yú at	庐 Lú hut	下 Xià below	见 Jiàn see	小 Xiǎo little	童 Tóng children
内 Nèi internal	息 Xī breath	思 Sī think	存 Cún keep	神 Shén spirit	明 Míng wisdom	光 Guāng light
出 Chū out	于 Yú of	天 Tiān heaven	门 Mén gate	入 Rù enter	无 Wú no	间 Jiàn space
恬 Tiān tranquil	淡 Dàn indifferent	无 Wú no	欲 Yù lust	养 Yǎng cultivate	华 Huá flowery	茎 Jīng stem

Two openings of the nostrils join the breath flow within the Yellow Court.

Exhale and inhale void within the void to see the own image.[18]

This will strengthen bones and tendons and make the blood pulse flourish.

In a profound state where outside world appears like non-existent, a blue spirit crosses over to itself.

Sitting at hut below you can see several little children[19].

Internal Qi breath would establish the wisdom light of spirit.

Looking within through a heavenly gate, in continuous in-flow,

Tranquil and calm, without lust, cultivate the inner Flower Sprout.

---

18) In this case, Yellow Court indicates Dan Tian. Inhales and exhales of the post-heaven breath initiate original (Yuan) Qi in the Dan Tian into a Pre-Heaven fetus breath.

19) Children are related to the new instances (spirit incarnations or the transformations) of the Individuality, that get formed one within the other, inheriting and enhancing Virtue from the previous existence,

Fú	Shí	Xuán	Qì	Kě	Suì	Shēng
服	食	玄	气	可	遂	生
take	eat	profound	energy	can	satisfy	life

Huán	Fǎn	Qī	Mén	Yǐn	Tài	Yuān
还	返	七	门	饮	太	渊
return		seven	gate	drink	ancient abyss	

Tōng	Wǒ	Xuán	Yīng	Guò	Qīng	Líng
通	我	玄	膺	过	清	灵
connect	own	mysterious	channel	cross	clear	spirit

Zuò	Yú	Yīng	Jiān	Jiàn	Xiǎo	Tóng
坐	于	膺	间	见	小	童
sit	at	chest	between	see	little children	

Wèn	Wǒ	Xiān	Dào	Yǔ	Qí	Fāng
问	我	仙	道	与	奇	方
ask	own	immortal	Tao	and	rare	method

Fú	Shí	Zǐ	Cǎo	Zǐ	Yù	Yīng
服	食	紫	草	紫	玉	英
take	eat	purple	mushroom	grass	Jade	Bravery

Tóu	Dài	Bái	Sù	Zú	Dān	Tián
头	戴	白	素	足	丹	田
head	wear	white	plain	foot	Dan	Tian

Mù	Yù	Huá	Chí	Shēng	Líng	Gēn
沐	浴	华	池	生	灵	根
bath		magnificent	pool	grow	Spirit Root	

Ingest the profound energy to satisfy life.

Return to seven gates a drink from the ancient abyss.

Connect to your mysterious source from above and let the clear spirit cross in.

There would be a little child[20], sitting at the chest.

Let it deliver your unique method of immortality in Tao.

Eat purple medicine mushroom to achieve a purple Jade Courage.

White light in front of the head is integrated to the essence of Earth coming from feet[21] to the Dan Tian.

Bathe in magnificent pool to nurture Spirit Root.

---

20) Stone-cutter Alchemist boy, giving away flecks of the Golden Inner light to the world, within the specific Big Dipper formations (see Figure 7, 9 and 11).

21) Kidney-1 acupuncture point (through two feet, symmetrically) integrates man to the Earth energies, spiritual light through the third eye integrates man to the Heavenly world. These two energies mix together in the middle, the center of the body geometry, the lower Dan Tian.

三府相得开命门
Sān Fǔ Xiāng Dé Kāi Mìng Mén
three mansion mutually gain open life gate

五味皆至善气还
Wǔ Wèi Jiē Zhì Shàn Qì Huán
five flavor all reach good energy return

大道荡荡心勿烦
Dà Dào Dàng Dàng Xīn Wù Fán
great Tao roam roam heart not troubled

披发行之可长存
Pī Fā Xíng Zhī Kě Cháng Cún
spread hair engage it can long last

吾言毕矣勿妄传。
Wú Yán Bì Yǐ Wù Wàng Chuán
my word finish do not recklessly spread

Three mansions cooperate to open the Life Gate.

Five flavors all merge to the central energy elixir.

Great Tao washes heart so it is not troubled.

Spread hair to engage the longevity formation[22].

The words of Jade Writing are thus complete, should not be spread in vain, but always honored.

---

22) Hair flow connects head and body to the Primordial Void.

Section II

Huáng   Tíng   Nèi   Jǐng   Jīng

黄   庭   内   景   经

Yellow   Court   Internal   Scenery   Scripture

Figure 11: Simplified "Internal Alchemy Pathways" scroll of the Qi flow and elixir transformation

Yellow Court Internal Scenery Scripture

This text has been preserved in Wang Xizhi tablets, and presents a superset of all the words from the External Scene Scripture. It is an "unfolded" version of the "enfolded" (high-level) story of the External Scene Scripture.

The abstraction and diversification of the units of meaning, which correspond to the holographic nature of the world, has been a common practice in the various spiritual traditions, e.g. in the acronym ICHTHUS (which enfolds the words "Iesous Christos Theou Huios Soter," Jesus Christ Son of God Savior) or in the Qabalah (where every letter represents a numeric series of meanings).

In addition to the obvious mnemonic benefits of the enfolded concepts, the unfolding and enfolding principle also helps bridging the gap between "big picture" and the focus areas of interest (meditation or practice). The self-inclusive meanings of the "Yellow Court" term itself are also the subject to this process (as described with Figure 6).

Different body subsystems are mostly presented in this Scripture by different palace sections, with the specific decoration (symbolizing its element and function), but also as planets, islands, mountains, valleys, and rivers. The spirits who govern them are characterized through different colors and material of the clothes or the regular duties.

The "Immortal Pathway" scroll, originated from the White Lotus temple (presented in a simplified draft on Figure 11) illustrates some of the symbolic landscapes mentioned in the Internal Scenery Scripture, along with the active agents who govern them. The upward flowing "Heavenly River" symbolizes the re-integration path (mentioned along with Figure 4 and Formula [1]), while the characters living at its banks, such as the Cowherd Boy, Weaving Maiden, and Stonecutter Alchemist (mentioned in the text) symbolize the nature of transformation at the specific points.

上清章第一

Shàng Qīng Zhāng Dì Yī
High Qing Chapter No. One

上 清 紫 霞 虚 皇 前
Shàng Qīng Zǐ Xiá Xū Huáng Qián
High Qing purple rosy cloud void emperor front

太 上 大 道 玉 晨 君。
Tài Shàng Dà Dào Yù Chén Jūn
ancient above great Tao jade morning gentleman

闲 居 蕊 珠 作 七 言
Xián Jū Ruǐ Zhū Zuò Qī Yán
idle live stamen pearl write seven stanza

散 化 五 形 变 万 神。
Sàn Huà Wǔ Xíng Biàn Wàn Shén
disperse transform five shape change 10,000 spirit

是 为 黄 庭 曰 内 篇
Shì Wéi Huáng Tíng Yuē Nèi Piān
is for yellow court say internal chapter

琴 心 三 叠 舞 胎 仙。
Qín Xīn Sān Dié Wǔ Tāi Xiān
qin (instrument) heart three tiers dance fetus fairy

九 气 映 明 出 霄 间
Jiǔ Qì Yìng Míng Chū Xiāo Jiān
nine energy shine brightness out cloud within

114

Chapter 2.1

In the Supreme Pure Realm,[1] in the Palace of Jade Pearls, enveloped by a Purple Cloud,

the Mystical and Ancient Great Dao Emperor of the Realm

created in his leisure time a seven-fold composition,[2]

that could change shape according to five forms and seed 10,000 divine archetypes,

composing the Inner Scripture of the Yellow Court.

The three-fold strings of its Qin[3] beat[4] the rhythm for a transcendental dance of the immortal embryo;

nine Qi[5] clear out clouds like sunshine,

---

1) Supreme Pure realm is one of the three Taoist Realms: Jade Purity, Supreme Purity, and Grand Purity, ruled by three legendary emperors. The emperor of Supreme Purity Realm is Ling Bao.

2) Each verse contains seven characters. "Leisure time" indicates Wu Wei (non-doing).

3) Qin is a seven-stringed Chinese musical instrument that has been played since ancient times.

4) Each string of the Qin can be segmented into three parts by the hands of the musician, thus creating three standing sound waves (see Figure 10). In the body, this structure corresponds to the three Dan Tian that structure its internal energy field.

5) Nine sounds can be generated by the musician's fingers that simultaneously play on three strings. In the human, body they correspond to three types of Qi in each Dan Tian, formed by their internal "spin" or "modes of time" (see the Introduction).

115

Shén	Gài	Tóng	Zǐ	Shēng	Zǐ	Yān
神	盖	童	子	生	紫	烟。
spirit	cover	boy	seed	high	purple	mist

Shì	Yuē	Yù	Shū	Kě	Jīng	Yán
是	曰	玉	书	可	精	研
it is	said	jade	book	can	deliberately	research

Yǒng	Zhī	Wàn	Guò	Shēng	Sān	Tiān
咏	之	万	过	升	三	天。
sing	it	tens of thousand times		rise	three days	

Qiān	Zāi	Yǐ	Xiāo	Bǎi	Bìng	Quán
千	灾	以	消	百	病	痊
1000	misfortune	therefore	dispel	100	diseases	heal

Bù	Dàn	Hǔ	Láng	Zhī	Xiōng	Cán
不	惮	虎	狼	之	凶	残
not	fear	tiger	wolf	's	fierce	cruel

Yì	Yǐ	Què	Lǎo	Nián	Yǒng	Yán
亦	以	却	老	年	永	延。
also	therefore	refuse	old	age	forever	elongate

and the spinout of Youth within the Divine form[6] generates a purple cloud.[7]

This scripture, also known as "Jade Writing," requires a serious study.

Chant it 10,000 times to ascend to the Three Pure Heavens,[8]

dispense 1,000 troubles and heal 100 diseases,

become immune even to the fierceness of a tiger and the cruelty of wolves,[9]

and be capable of refusing aging forever.

---

6) Youth born within the Divine indicates a spirit process, a seamlessly paradoxical principle, to initiate a new mission of virtue in a temporal world, while residing beyond it. illustrated in The Jade Emperor Mind Seal Classic words 存无守有, 倾刻而成, "reside in non-being while cultivating being, to achieve perfection" illustrates the same concept, as well David Bohm's "holonomy" (transformation in which a new whole is emerging) concept in quantum physics.

7) Purple mist symbolizes the Spirit Truth or "Akasha record" (or the "world sheet" made by superstring vibration). According to legend, purple mist also accompanied Lao Zi on his journey to the west, to spread the teachings of the Tao.

8) Three Purity Realms, as in 1).

9) Tiger symbolizes giving up one's Uniqueness to the complete dissolution in "One", while wolves symbolize dissipating one's connection with Oneness for "Many" disintegrated components. The true seat of Individuality is in between, as in the metaphor presented in "Yi Jing": "A True Man doesn't subject himself either to One (king), or Many (nobles), as his path is higher than that."

上 有 章 第 二

Shàng 上 Above — Yǒu 有 Exists — Zhāng 章 Chapter — Dì 第 No. — Èr 二 Two

Shàng 上	Yǒu 有	Hún 魂	Líng 灵	Xià 下	Guān 关	Yuán 元
above	exists	soul	spirit	below	junction	origin

Zuǒ 左	Wéi 为	Shǎo 少	Yáng 阳	Yòu 右	Tài 太	Yīn 阴。
left	is	young	Yang	right	old	Yin.

Hòu 后	Yǒu 有	Mì 密	Hù 户	Qián 前	Shēng 生	Mén 门。
behind	exists	secret	door	front	birth	gate

Chū 出	Rì 日	Rù 入	Yuè 月	Hū 呼	Xī 吸	Cún 存。
exhale	sun	inhale	moon	breath out	breath in	deposit

Sì 四	Qì 气	Suǒ 所	Hé 合	Liè 列	Sù 宿	Fēn 分
four	Qi	therefore	join	arrange	night	separate

Zǐ 紫	Yān 烟	Shàng 上	Xià 下	Sān 三	Sù 素	Yún 云。
purple	mist	above	below	three	plain	cloud

Guàn 灌	Gài 溉	Wǔ 五	Huá 华	Zhí 植	Líng 灵	Gēn 根
irrigate		five	splendid	plant	spirit	root

118

Chapter 2.2

Eternal Spirit is above, the Gate of Origin[1] is below.

Young Yang[2] is on the left, Old Yin[3] is on the right.

Secret Door[4] is behind; Door of Creation[5] is at the front.

Exhale with Sun, inhale with Moon, cultivating the breath.

The four phases of new Qi blend together, non-integrated old Qi flows out.[6]

A purple steam rises and descends between the three clouds,[7] infusing its essence to the five internal organs and root of the Spirit.

---

1) Guan Yuan or "Gate or Origin," point CV-4, represents the junction between inner and outer storage of the primordial essence.

2) Xiao Yang , or Young Yang, represents Spring, East, or Wood.

3) Tai Yin, or Old Yin, represents Winter, North, or Water.

4) Ming Men is a Secret Door point at the back of the body, opposite the navel.

5) Sheng Men is the Door of Creation and represents the navel.

6) This verse describes a main principle of this chapter, called "fostering yang, repelling yin," the practice of "walking with Tao," acting on renewal and continuous improvement of temporal reality, an alchemy step in actualization of "Zhen Ren" (True Man).

7) Qi flows through the Microcosmic Orbit; while its five phases nurture different organs.

七 液 洞 流 冲 庐 间。
Qī Yè Dòng Liú Chōng Lú Jiān
seven fluid cave flow flush hut in the middle

回 紫 抱 黄 入 丹 田
Huí Zǐ Bào Huáng Rù Dān Tián
circulate purple hold yellow in Dan Tian

幽 室 内 明 照 阳 门。
Yōu Shì Nèi Míng Zhào Yáng Mén
dark room internal bright shine yang gate.

Seven liquids flow through without obstacle and integrate in the central Yellow Palace.[8]

Circulate Purple and embrace Yellow[9] in the Dan Tian

and Yang Light of the Spirit will illuminate the darkness around.[10]

---

8) Waves of seven emotions/frequencies (like colors of the spectrum) blend together in the geometrical and gravity center of the body (the lower Dan Tian) to produce the holistic reflection (holographic picture) of the world.

9) "Purple" indicates Yang, movement, eternal (self) perfection, continual ingestion of the new wisdom. "Yellow" represents Yin, centralized peaceful seat of the Spirit, the observation point of the perception.

10) Renewed Spirit becomes like a living Star in one's own space of Mystery.

Kǒu	Wéi	Zhāng	Dì	Sān
口	为	章	第	三
Mouth	Is	Chapter	No.	Three

Kǒu	Wéi	Yù	Chí	Tài	Hé	Guān
口	为	玉	池	太	和	官。
mouth	is	jade	pool	ancient	peace	organ.

Shù	Yān	Líng	Yè	Zāi	Bù	Gān
漱	咽	灵	液	灾	不	干。
gargle	throat	effective	liquid	disaster	not	dry

Tǐ	Shēng	Guāng	Huá	Qì	Xiāng	Lán
体	生	光	华	气	香	兰
body	produces	light	splendid	Qi	fragrance	orchid

Què	Miè	Bǎi	Xié	Yù	Liàn	Yán
却	灭	百	邪	玉	炼	颜。
yet	extinguish	hundreds	evil	jade	refine	appearance

Shěn	Néng	Xiū	Zhī	Dēng	Guǎng	Hán
审	能	修	之	登	广	寒。
examine	able	repair	it	climb	broad	coldness

Zhòu	Yè	Bù	Mèi	Nǎi	Chéng	Zhēn
昼	夜	不	寐	乃	成	真
day	night	not	sleep	therefore	become	true

Léi	Míng	Diàn	Jī	Shén	Mǐn	Mǐn
雷	鸣	电	激	神	泯	泯。
thunder	sound		lightning	spirit	vanish	submerge

Chapter 2.3

The mouth is the Jade Pool of Ancient Peace.

Rinse and gulp the precious dew to prevent drying.[1]

The body will generate fragrance and splendor.

Hundreds of diseases will be extinguished, and the form
will be like refined jade.

Rediscover and reform yourself and climb to the Lunar
Palace.[2]

Do not attach to day or night, and you will achieve
existence in Truth.[3]

You will stay tranquil even in the midst of powerful
thunders and lightning.[4]

---

1) The "water wheel" cycle in the human body replenishes itself in
the upper Dan Tian (the source of the "rain" of saliva enriched
by the Qi generated in mouth) and the lower Dan Tian (the
source of "steam" of internally generated energy empowered by
the Earth energy).

2) Lunar Palace signifies the target state of each cycle where man
accomplishes calm and continual presence in Truth, sharing the
global consciousness (see the outer edge of Compass, Figure 9).

3) Describes the principle of "uniting Yin and Yang" (a reflection of
the Tao in eternal reality), A practitioner ascends to a place of
peace outside of Yin-Yang changes.

4) An inner peace in the pivot point of IE symmetry (see the Figure
2) cannot be disturbed by any causal or sympathetic influence
from the domain of non-integrated opposites. Thunder
symbolizes causal (longitudinal wave pattern) transfer of
influence, Lightning symbolizes synchronistic (see the works of
C. G. Jung), indirect influence (transferred through a transversal
wave pattern).

黄庭章第四
Huáng Tíng Zhāng Dì Sì

Yellow Court Chapter No. Four

黄庭内人服锦衣
Huáng Tíng Nèi Rén Fú Jǐn Yī

yellow court in people clothe brocade clothes

紫华飞裙云气罗。
Zǐ Huá Fēi Qún Yún Qì Luó

purple splendid fly dress cloud energy include

丹青绿条翠灵柯。
Dān Qīng Lǜ Tiáo Cuì Líng Kē

red fresh green stripes green spirit branch

七蕤玉龠闭两扉
Qī Ruí Yù Yuè Bì Liǎng Fēi

seven flowers jade flute close two head page

重扇金关密枢机。
Zhòng Shàn Jīn Guān Mì Shū Jī

multiple fans gold pass secret hinge hub

玄泉幽阙高崔巍
Xuán Quán Yōu Què Gāo Cuī Wēi

profound spring secluded barrier high mountain lofty

三田之中精气微。
Sān Tián Zhī Zhōng Jīng Qì Wēi

three field 's middle essence Qi subtle

Chapter 2.4

Courtiers of the Yellow Castle are all clothed in silk brocade,[1]

a splendid purple flying robe that has been woven with cloud Qi.[2]

Its red and green seams are numinous boughs of the Spirit.

A jade wedge with seven flowers keeps secured the two-wing door.

The gold panels seal the windows of the castle halls.[3]

The walls around profound spring are strong and powerful,

in order to guard the sublimation of the essence flowing through the centers of the three fields.[4]

---

1) "Silk-woven brocade," used throughout the text, is associated with personal fine clothing or room draperies. Long silk threads symbolize the rays of sunlight. Numinousity indicate a presence of the mystical principle.

2) Purple flying robe indicates the richness of the spiritual information. Clouds indicate a high refinement of the cultivated Jing that can be used for alchemical purposes.

3) The apertures of the body are safely guarded against any disturbance.

4) The Chong Mai vessel, where the heavenly river flows, carrying Qi upward through the middle of the body, connecting the three Dan Tian (see Figure 11), is strong and without leaks, enabling a powerful purification process.

娇 女 窈 窕 翳 霄 晖

Jiāo lovely / Nǚ girl / Yǎo fair / Tiǎo ladies / Yì conceal / Xiāo cloud / Huī sunshine

重 堂 焕 焕 明 八 威。

Zhòng multiple / Táng hall / Huàn Huàn glowing / Míng brighten / Bā eight / Wēi power

天 庭 地 关 列 斧 斤

Tiān heaven / Tíng court / Dì earth / Guān pass / Liè list / Fǔ hatchet / Jīn pound

灵 台 盘 固 永 不 衰。

Líng soul / Tái platform / Pán form / Gù solid / Yǒng forever / Bù no / Shuāi wane

Delicate beauty shines through a screen of clouds.[5]

Internal halls glow, illuminated by the eight powers.[6]

The arms are aligned in order, from the heavenly court to the earthly fortification.[7]

The castle of the soul doesn't weaken and stays solid forever.[8]

---

5) Internal light appears before the eyes with almost closed eyelids in meditation, like sunshine from clouds.

6) Eight-fold (trigram) change by the light of creation is directed within.

7) Aligning the coordination of the whole body from head to feet, as in the ancient quote: "If the energy circulates from the center to the extremities, one will remain in perfect health."

8) In the process where "Shen is gathered within and Qi is excited and radiated without" (a quote from Zhang San Feng's Tai Chi classic), the body gets a Tao foundation. This can be achieved only by diligently combining mental introspection and energetic exercise. This illustrates the principle of "transcending Yin and Yang," where the cycle of action is reactivated but now driven indirectly ("Wu Wei"), without direct engagement of the practitioner. This step completes the "fostering yang, repelling yin" and "uniting yin and yang" sequence in the formulation of the practitioner's vision of the "Zhen Ren" state (divinity or a true self).

Zhōng	Chí	Zhāng	Dì	Wǔ
中	池	章	第	五
Middle	Pool	Chapter	No. Five	

Zhōng	Chí	Nèi	Shén	Fú	Chì	Zhū
中	池	内	神	服	赤	珠
middle	pool	internal	spirit	take	red	pearl

Dān	Jǐn	Yún	Páo	Dài	Hǔ	Fú
丹	锦	云	袍	带	虎	符。
red	brocade	cloud	gown	with	tiger	symbol

Héng	Jīn	Sān	Cùn	Líng	Suǒ	Jū
横	津	三	寸	灵	所	居
across	saliva	three	inch	soul	where	lives

Yǐn	Zhī	Yì	Yù	Zì	Xiāng	Fú
隐	芝	翳	郁	自	相	扶。
concealed	glossy ganoderma	veiled	fragrance		each other	foster

Chapter 2.5

The middle pool of the internal spirit bathes the red pearl.[1]

The red brocade gown of divinity hides the mark of the tiger.[2]

In strong liquid, three inches from the residence of the soul,

hidden core energies foster each other.[3]

---

1) Red indicates the element of fire and the heart, the place of the middle Dan Tian.

2) Dragon is a symbol of descending Heart Qi (trigram Li, fire). Tiger symbolizes ascending Kidney Qi (trigram Kan, water). The mark of the tiger indicates the acquired ability to create Qi steam from Jing liquid.

3) The body thrives when the energies of Kan and Li interchange their nature and complement each other, i.e., fire sinks down like rain while water rises up like steam.

天 中 章 第 六

Tiān — 天 — Heaven
Zhōng — 中 — Middle
Zhāng — 章 — Chapter
Dì — 第 — No. Six
Liù — 六

Tiān 天 heaven	Zhōng 中 middle	Zhī 之 's	Yuè 岳 mountain	Jīng 精 essence	Jǐn 谨 solemnly	Xiū 修 built
Yún 云 cloud	Zhái 宅 mansion	Jì 既 since	Qīng 清 quiet	Yù 玉 jade	Dì 帝 emperor	Yóu 游。 visit
Tōng 通 knowledge	Lì 利 advantage	Dào 道 Tao	Lù 路 pathway	Wú 无 no	Zhōng 终 endpoint	Xiū 休 rest
Méi 眉 eyebrow	Hào 号 ordinal	Huá 华 canopy	Gài 盖 covered	Fù 覆 shining	Míng 明	Zhū 珠。 pearls
Jiǔ 九 nine	Yōu 幽 dark	Rì 日 sun	Yuè 月 moon	Dòng 洞 empty	Kōng 空 air	Wú 无 none

Chapter 2.6

The nose is like a high mountain in the middle of Heaven,

its root is like a mansion that hosts the quiet visits of the Jade Emperor.[1]

Knowledge advances along this path without end.

Between the eyebrows, an imperial canopy covers a shining pearl,

illuminating, without interruption, the nine hidden caves of the Upper Dan Tian.[2]

---

1) The gate of Spirit, between the eyebrows, where essence is breathed in.

2) According to Taoist teachings, there are nine palaces residing in the Upper Dan Tian ("Mud Ball", Ni Wan, or brain); the first one is mentioned above. They reflect he external "four-dimensional bodies" (mentioned in the Introduction) that flow to each other without breaks. With the presence of Spirit, they shine with life, which is externally physically noticeable by the sparks in the practitioner's eyes.

Zhái	Zhōng	Yǒu	Zhēn	Cháng	Yī	Dān
宅	中	有	真	常	衣	丹。
house	in	there is	true	constant	clothe	pellet

Shěn	Néng	Jiàn	Zhī	Wú	Jí	Huàn
审	能	见	之	无	疾	患
examine	can	see	it	without	sickness	suffer

Chì	Zhū	Líng	Qún	Huá	Qiàn	Càn
赤	珠	灵	裙	华	茜	粲。
red	pearl	fairy	gown	splendid	luxuriant	beaming

Shé	Xià	Xuán	Yīng	Shēng	Sǐ	Ǎn
舌	下	玄	膺	生	死	岸
tongue	below	dark	bear	life	death	bank

Chū	Qīng	Rù	Xuán	Èr	Qì	Huàn
出	青	入	玄	二	气	焕
exist	green	enter	darkness	two	energy	glowing

Zǐ	Ruò	Yù	Zhī	Shēng	Tiān	Hàn
子	若	遇	之	升	天	汉。
son	if	meet	it	rise	heaven	man

In the middle of the house lies the genuine eternal cinnabar chamber.[3]

Study it and you will find no imperfection.

The red pearl beams at its front magnificently.[4]

The tongue below embraces the shore of life and death.[5]

Renewal of life rises to enter mystery, joining the brilliant double Qi.[6]

Swallow the created essence and ascend to the Milky Way[7].

---

3) The medial of nine palaces, the "Celestial Palace" is the most holy place in the upper Dan Tian, where the spirit of Individuality (Yang Shen) resides. Cinnabar symbolizes the active spirit of intelligence.

4) At the front of the point where tongue (red, fire organ where the heart opens out) touches the upper palate during meditation, the "Immortal Pathway" scroll shows the red pearl of the heavenly elixir that integrates heaven and earth.

5) Underneath the tongue there is the Spring of Saliva (Xuan Ying), or Shore of Life and Death.

6) Gold (Yang) and Jade (Yin) fluid, rich with Qi, from the left and right salivary gland, mix, along with food, drink, and inhaled Qi, to provide nutrition and renewal for the body.

7) Ingest the rain of divine plenty and it would be complemented by the steam rising through the spinal cord (symbolized by the Milky Way or Heavenly River on Figure 11). This also corresponds to a principle of the integration of Oneness with the world in the physical existence and, in a complementary flow, ascension of the Personal Consciousness to the spiritual realm.

至 道 章 第 七
Zhì Dào Zhāng Dì Qī
Utmost Tao Chapter No. Seven

Zhì	Dào	Bù	Fán	Jué	Cún	Zhēn
至	道	不	烦	决	存	真
utmost	Tao	not	trouble	determination	exist	truth

Ní	Wán	Bǎi	Jié	Jiē	Yǒu	Shén
泥	丸	百	节	皆	有	神。
mud	ball	hundred	section	all	has	spirit

Fā	Shén	Cāng	Huá	Zì	Tài	Yuán
发	神	苍	华	字	太	元
hair	spirit	blue	splendid	style name	ancient	beginning

Nǎo	Shén	Jīng	Gēn	Zì	Ní	Wán
脑	神	精	根	字	泥	丸
brain	spirit	essence	root	style name	mud	ball

Yǎn	Shén	Míng	Shàng	Zì	Yīng	Xuán
眼	神	明	上	字	英	玄
eye	spirit	bright	above	style name	profound	mystery

Bí	Shén	Yù	Lǒng	Zì	Líng	Jiān
鼻	神	玉	垄	字	灵	坚
nose	spirit	jade	ridge	style name	spirit	solid

Ěr	Shén	Kōng	Xián	Zì	Yōu	Tián
耳	神	空	闲	字	幽	田
ear	spirit	leisure		style name	serene	field

Chapter 2.7

Achieve Tao, do not try to determine what is real.

Every section of the brain has an inherent spiritual divinity.

The dark blue hair spirit is known as an "Ancient Origin."[1]

The essential brain spirit is known as a "Mud Ball."[2]

The bright eye spirit is known as "Exploring the Mystery."[3]

The jade nose peak spirit is known as "Resolute Efficiency."

The relaxed spirit of the ear is known as a "Quiet Field."

---

1) According to various ancient teachings, hair connects us to the source of our youth and strength. (Taoists, as opposed to Buddhists, keep the hair long, to symbolize aspirations to the longevity of the body and integration with the individual non-being.)

2) The term Ni Wan ("Mud Ball"), one of the synonyms for Huang Ting ("Yellow Court"), is used for either the central chamber of the brain or the whole of the brain and is considered as the material base of the Spirit, or the "field of mystery" in which it resides in its specific incarnation. Brain cells differ from the other cell types in the body because they are the only ones that persist during life (vertical, asymmetry line of TC symmetry), while the other cells recycle (symmetry, horizontal axis) in about a month or less.

3) "Tao Te Ching" Chapter 1 refers to (玄之又玄, Mystery within Mystery, indicated the same word as in "Ying Xuan". Mystery according to Taoist teachings is infinite and in the constant interplay with the Truth.

舌	神	通	命	字	正	伦
Shé	Shén	Tōng	Mìng	Zì	Zhèng	Lún
tongue	spirit	know	fate	style name	main	ethics

齿	神	峭	峰	字	罗	千。
Chǐ	Shén	Qiào	Fēng	Zì	Luó	Qiān
tooth	spirit	cliff	peak	style name	including	thousands

一	面	之	神	宗	泥	丸
Yī	Miàn	Zhī	Shén	Zōng	Ní	Wán
one	face	's	spirit	model	mud	ball

泥	丸	九	真	皆	有	房。
Ní	Wán	Jiǔ	Zhēn	Jiē	Yǒu	Fáng
mud	ball	nine	truth	all	has	house

方	圆	一	寸	处	此	中
Fāng	Yuán	Yī	Cùn	Chǔ	Cǐ	Zhōng
circumference		one	inch	reside	this	center

同	服	紫	衣	飞	罗	裳。
Tóng	Fú	Zǐ	Yī	Fēi	Luó	Cháng
same	clothe	purple	clothes	fly	silk	robe

但	思	一	部	寿	无	穷
Dàn	Sī	Yī	Bù	Shòu	Wú	Qióng
once	meditate	one	part	longevity	no	end

非	各	别	住	俱	脑	中。
Fēi	Gè	Bié	Zhù	Jù	Nǎo	Zhōng
not	each	other	reside	entirely	brain	between

136

The magical spirit of the tongue is known as "True Coherence."

The vanguard spirit of the teeth is known as "Strong Multitude."

All divinities that are expressed on a face have their origin in the "Mud Ball."

The nine truths of the mud ball all have a house

in circumference of one inch from the center.

Its tapestry is made from the purple silk flying robe.[4]

Meditate on just central section, and your longevity will have no end.

These rooms do not reside fully in the brain.

They are all part of external reality,

which reflects in mind and vice versa.[5]

---

4) Silk symbolizes sunlight; the purple color symbolizes spirit presence in different time modes. The connection of the nine rooms (see Figure 8) indicates the simultaneous existence in different modalities, which transform to each other by passing the light to shadow and vice versa (transitions can be mapped by a sequence of Yin/Yang state changes of the trigrams that correspond to the four-dimensional bodies of an Individual).

5) Two common perceptions reality, world in the mind (scientific) and mind in the world (magical), are just different projections of the true integral presence. See comment above and Figure 8 for a description of nine palaces of the mind.

Xīn 心 Heart	**Shén** 神 Spirit	**Zhāng** 章 Chapter	**Dì** 第	**Bā** 八 No. Eight

Xīn 心 heart	**Shén** 神 spirit	**Dān** 丹 red	**Yuán** 元 origin	**Zì** 字 style name	**Shǒu** 守 guard	**Líng** 灵 soul
Fèi 肺 lung	**Shén** 神 spirit	**Hào** 皓 luminous	**Huá** 华 splendid	**Zì** 字 style name	**Xū** 虚 void	**Chéng** 成。 form
Gān 肝 liver	**Shén** 神 spirit	**Lóng** 龙 dragon	**Yān** 烟 mist	**Zì** 字 style name	**Hán** 含 contain	**Míng** 明 wisdom
Yì 翳 opacity	**Yù** 郁 stagnancy	**Dǎo** 导 direct	**Yān** 烟 smoke	**Zhǔ** 主 indicate	**Zhuó** 浊 obstruction	**Qīng** 清。 clear
Shèn 肾 kidney	**Shén** 神 spirit	**Xuán** 玄 dark	**Míng** 冥 underworld	**Zì** 字 style name	**Yù** 育 nurture	**Yīng** 婴 infant
Pí 脾 spleen	**Shén** 神 spirit	**Cháng** 常 always	**Zài** 在 exist	**Zì** 字 style name	**Hún** 魂 soul	**Tíng** 停。 stop
Dǎn 胆 gallbladder	**Shén** 神 spirit	**Lóng** 龙 dragon	**Yào** 曜 glorious	**Zì** 字 style name	**Wēi** 威 mighty	**Míng** 明。 bright

138

Chapter 2.8

The primordial cinnabar spirit of the heart is known as the "Soul Guardian."[1]

The splendid luminous spirit of the lungs is known as "Void Formation."

The Liver Spirit in dragon mist is known as the "Keeper of Wisdom."

Its dense screens filter out all the impurities.[2]

The dark spirit of the kidneys lying below is known as "Embryo Nurturing."

The continually existing Spleen Spirit is known as the "Haven of the Soul."[3]

The dragon spirit of the gall bladder is known as "Powerful Brightness."[4]

---

1) "Hun" spirit of heart, which helps maintain high achievement of the soul (gradient tangent at the max extreme on Figure 5).

2) In both TCM and western medical science the liver regulates the precise chemical balance of the body health.

3) Spleen corresponds to the element Earth (that connects different cycles of the four other phases - seasons) and to a turnaround point of any transformation at 360 degrees (see Figure 5). The related Natural principle or Spirit reflects the synchronicity of the existence in all phases.

4) Both liver and gall bladder are associated with East, Wood, and "Green Dragon." Yang Gall bladder embodies that nature of all other Yang (6 Fu) organs to pass through fluids and energy, "light".

Liù	Fǔ	Wǔ	Cáng	Shén	Tǐ	Jīng
六	腑	五	藏	神	体	精
six	hollow organs	five	solid organs	spirit	body	essence

Jiē	Zài	Xīn	Nèi	Yùn	Tiān	Jīng
皆	在	心	内	运	天	经。
all	located	heart	in	operate	heaven	scripture

Zhòu	Yè	Cún	Zhī	Zì	Cháng	Shēng
昼	夜	存	之	自	长	生。
day	night	keep	it	oneself	long	longevity

Six hollow organs and five solid organs provide essence for the body and soul.[5]

Their spirits operate in concord with the heavenly scriptures.[6]

Maintain this order all day and night to achieve longevity.

---

5) The six hollow "Fu" organs are: large intestine, urinary bladder, gall bladder, small intestine, stomach, and triple warmer (San Jiao). The five solid "Zang" organs are: lungs, kidneys, liver, heart (pericardium and heart are considered a single organ), and spleen.

6) Heavenly scriptures (like the present one), of assumed Divine Origin, aspire to reintegrate external and internal aspects of the practitioner, describing how Qi from without can be collected in the body until it radiates out in a new way. Zang (storage organs) keep the Qi, while the Fu (hollow) organs pass it through, each in its specific way.

肺 部 章 第 九

Fèi 肺 Lung　**Bù** 部 Part　**Zhāng** 章 Chapter　**Dì** 第　**Jiǔ** 九 No. Nine

Fèi	Bù	Zhī	Gōng	Sì	Huá	Gài
肺	部	之	宫	似	华	盖
lung	part	of	palace	similar	splendid	cover

Xià	Yǒu	Tóng	Zǐ	Zuò	Yù	Què
下	有	童	子	坐	玉	阙。
below	there is	child	boy	sit	jade	watchtower

Qī	Yuán	Zhī	Zǐ	Zhǔ	Diào	Qì
七	元	之	子	主	调	气
seven	element	's	son	chief	adjust	Qi

Wài	Yīng	Zhōng	Yuè	Bí	Qí	Wèi
外	应	中	岳	鼻	齐	位。
external	respond	middle	mount	nose	even	position

Sù	Jǐn	Yī	Cháng	Huáng	Yún	Dài
素	锦	衣	裳	黄	云	带
plain	brocade	clothes	garment	yellow	cloud	scarf

Chuǎn	Xī	Hū	Xī	Tǐ	Bù	Kuài
喘	息	呼	吸	体	不	快。
	breathe	exhale	inhale	body	not	well

Jí	Cún	Bái	Yuán	Hé	Liù	Qì
急	存	白	元	和	六	气
urgent	save	white	chief	and	six	Qi

142

Chapter 2.9

The Lung section of the palace[1] resembles an imperial canopy.

Underneath sits a divine stonecutter boy on a jade watchtower.[2]

The Qi is transformed at the base of seven stars.[3]

Externally the lungs open to the nose, which stands in the center of the face, as the Mt. Song.[4]

It wears snow-white brocade, with a yellow belt floating like a cloud.[5]

Breathe deeply if body doesn't feel well, rigorously absorbing the white essence of the six flows[6].

---

1) The palace symbolizes the body.

2) According to Taoist symbolic body landscape, below the lungs and the heart there is a youth alchemist/stonecutter divinity (Huo Hua), who preserves Spirit by spreading transmuted gold (Qi generated from Jing) into the firmament of heaven (symbolizing good deeds).

3) Seven stars formed in the firmament (that also map to seven openings of the head and the heart) are arranged into the form of the Great Northern Dipper, from which flows Cinnabar (Yang Qi) from a Great Cosmic source to regenerate the Spirit (by transmutation from Qi).

4) Mt. Song is one of the five sacred mountains,

5) Lungs (corresponding to Metal and white color) organ is the "child" of the spleen (associated with the element of earth and the color yellow) in the theory of Five Organs (Figure 5).

6) The six flows, permeated by a breath essence (white for metal element) are: essence, energy, saliva, body, blood, and pulse.

Shén	Xiān	Jiǔ	Shì	Wú	Zāi	Hài
神	仙	久	视	无	灾	害。
spirit	fairy	long	watch	no	disaster	harm

Yòng	Zhī	Bù	Yǐ	Xíng	Bù	Zhì
用	之	不	已	形	不	滞。
use	it	without	already	shape	no	stagnant

An immortal spirit watches carefully to avoid leaks of Qi

and avoid its stagnation, during its flow anywhere in the field of existence.[7]

---

7) The "Identity Field" or the Individual Void Qi is led by mind, so it goes to any internal or external corner of our world we can imagine. The strength of its presence depends on the focus of the practitioner, but it can definitely cause reciprocal change in our presence in the world.

Xīn 心 Heart	Bù 部 part	Zhāng 章 Chapter	Dì 第	Shí 十 No. Ten		

Xīn 心 heart	Bù 部 part	Zhī 之 of	Gōng 宫 palace	Lián 莲 lotus	Hán 含 contain	Huá 华 essence
Xià 下 below	Yǒu 有 there is	Tóng 童 virgin	Zǐ 子 boy	Dān 丹 red	Yuán 元 chief	Jiā 家。 house
Zhǔ 主 mainly	Shì 适 suit	Hán 寒 cold fever	Rè 热 heat	Róng 荣 honor	Wèi 卫 guard	Hé 和 harmony
Dān 丹 elixir/red	Jǐn 锦 brocade	Fēi 飞 flying	Cháng 裳 clothes	Pī 披 wear	Yù 玉 jade	Luó 罗。 silk
Jīn 金 gold	Líng 铃 bell	Zhū 朱 red	Dài 带 scarf	Zuò 坐 sit	Pó 婆 dancing	Zī 姿 beauty
Diào 调 adjust	Xuè 血 blood	Lǐ 理 manage	Mìng 命 life	Shēn 身 body	Bù 不 not	Kū 枯 wither
Wài 外 external	Yīng 应 respond	Kǒu 口 mouth	Shé 舌 tongue	Tǔ 吐 vomit	Wǔ 五 five	Huá 华。 essence

Chapter 2.10

The Heart section of the palace resembles a blossomed lotus flower full of essence.

Underneath sits a virgin[1] boy, the chief of the red house,

regulating the thriving harmony of the intertwined heat and cold.

He wears flying clothes[2] of silk brocade with jade ornaments,[3]

with a gold bell ringing and a red scarf dancing around.[3]

Adjust the blood flow in the rhythm of eternal life, and the body will not wither.

The heart opens to the mouth and tongue to taste the five essences.

---

1) Virgin youth in this verse represents the alchemy agent that regulates transformation of Qi to Shen.

2) Flight indicates transcendence, connection to the higher realms.

3) Silk represents Qi flow, jade represents continuity.

4) "Gold bell" symbolizes the heart beat, while "red scarf" symbolizes the smooth flow of blood.

Lín	Jué	Hū	Zhī	Yì	Dēng	Sū
临	绝	呼	之	亦	登	苏
just	never	exhaust	it	and	reach	revival

Jiǔ	Jiǔ	Xíng	Zhī	Fēi	Tài	Xiá
久	久	行	之	飞	太	霞。
long	long	walk	it	fly	ancient	rosy cloud

When the essences are spent out, exhale to enable revival.[4]

Practice diligently, to fly with ancient rosy clouds.[5]

---

4) The five essences are continually integrating in the body, but non-integrating parts need to go out in each cycle, to make place for fresh tidal wave.

5) The refined (cloud) essence of the Fire element (rose color) can be directed toward various transformations.

肝 部 章 第 十 一
Liver Part Chapter No. Eleven

肝 部 之 中 翠 重 里
liver part 's middle emerald heavy internal

下 有 青 童 神 公 子。
below there green virgin spirit male child

主 诸 关 键 聪 明 始
mainly all pass key intelligence bright start

青 锦 披 裳 佩 玉 铃。
green brocade wrap skirt wear jade bell

和 制 魂 魄 津 液 平
mixture produce spirit soul body fluid balanced

外 应 眼 目 日 月 清。
external respond pupil eye sun moon clear

百 疴 不 钟 存 无 英
hundred illness none time exist liver function

Chapter 2.11

The liver section of the castle is in the middle, resembling a green emerald.[1]

Underneath seats a virgin boy directing the green light and leading the key intelligence of the body processes.[2]

He wears green brocade and carries a jade bell.

His office arranges Yin and Yang Qi to balance body fluids,

opens externally in one's eyes that shine like the sun and moon,[3]

and regulates liver function, so that a hundred illnesses will cease to exist.[4]

---

1) Green is the symbolic color of the wood element and of the matching organs: liver and gall bladder. Emerald symbolizes the Moon, the source of Inner Light.

2) The physical liver also performs the most significant and complex chemical reactions in the body.

3) According to TCM, the liver is connected to external senses through the eyes. They process pictures of the world in a similar way as the liver processes internal nutrients.

4) Sun indicates the Spirit shining in, Moon indicates individual Spirit shining out. When body gets purified by this light flow, al imperfections and impurities will disappear.

Tóng	Yòng	Qī	Rì	Zì	Chōng	Yíng
同	用	七	日	自	充	盈。
together	use	seven	days	self	fulfillment	surplus

Chuí	Jué	Niàn	Shén	Sǐ	Fù	Shēng
垂	绝	念	神	死	复	生
drop	death	recite	god	death	return	life

Shè	Hún	Huán	Pò	Yǒng	Wú	Qīng
摄	魂	还	魄	永	无	倾。
transport	heaven soul	return	earth soul	forever	no	ending

Meditate on the Truth of the five viscera[4] for seven days.

Your spirit will be renewed and death will drop out.

The soul will return to its origin and find eternity.

---

4) The viscera, or the Zang organs, are: lungs, kidneys, liver, heart, and spleen. Each can embody, in its specific way, the specific types of the transformation of Qi ("light"), as on Figure 5, that clears the impurities and aging (which occurs if the light of the Sun is overused and one's own light is not created).

肾 部 章 第 十 二

Shèn Bù Zhāng Dì Shí Èr

Kidney Part Chapter No. Twelve

肾	部	之	宫	玄	阙	圆
Shèn	Bù	Zhī	Gōng	Xuán	Què	Yuán
kidney	section	's	palace	dark	watchtower	place

中	有	童	子	冥	上	玄。
Zhōng	Yǒu	Tóng	Zǐ	Míng	Shàng	Xuán
middle	there is	virgin	boy	dark	above	obscure

主	诸	六	府	九	液	源
Zhǔ	Zhū	Liù	Fǔ	Jiǔ	Yè	Yuán
mainly	all	six	residence	nine	fluid	source

外	应	两	耳	百	液	津。
Wài	Yīng	Liǎng	Ěr	Bǎi	Yè	Jīn
external	respond	two	ears	hundred	body	fluid

苍	锦	云	衣	舞	龙	幡
Cāng	Jǐn	Yún	Yī	Wǔ	Lóng	Fān
blue	brocade	cloud	clothed	dance	dragon	flag

上	致	明	霞	日	月	烟。
Shàng	Zhì	Míng	Xiá	Rì	Yuè	Yān
above	reach	bright	rosy cloud	sun	moon	mist

百	病	千	灾	当	急	存
Bǎi	Bìng	Qiān	Zāi	Dāng	Jí	Cún
hundred	illness	thousand	disasters	shall	urgent	survive

Chapter 2.12

The part of the palace dedicated to the Kidneys is like a dark watchtower place.[1]

In its center sits a virgin boy in profound darkness and mystery.[2]

The sources of all nine fluids are restored here.

Externally the office of the Kidneys is open to the ears, hearing and monitoring hundreds of pulses.

He is clothed in white silk that flows like a dragon dancing in the clouds.

When Kidney Qi ascends, it nourishes the brain

and shines like the sun and moon in rosy clouds.

The hundred diseases and thousand problems will disappear.

---

1) The color of the water element and its corresponding organs, kidney and urinary bladder, is black.

2) Kidney essence connects body of a person to the Pre-Heaven (pre-natal) existence.

两 部 水 王 对 生 门
Liǎng Bù Shuī Wáng Duì Shēng Mén
two ministry water king across life gate

使 人 长 生 升 九 天。
Shǐ Rén Cháng Shēng Shēng Jiǔ Tiān
make people long life ascend ninth heaven

Through the action of two water Kings across the life gate,[3]

a long life and ascendance to the ninth heaven is made
possible.

---

3) The two Kings (or rather the King in the left Kidney and the
Queen in the right) symbolize the centers of the Yin and Yang
potential of the Jing of the person (cultivated between Kidneys),
which is the root of all substance of the body.

脾 部 章 第 十 三

Pí	Bù	Zhāng	Dì	Shí	Sān
脾	部	章	第	十	三
Spleen	Section	Chapter		No. Thirteen	

Pí	Bù	Zhī	Gōng	Shǔ	Wù	Yǐ
脾	部	之	宫	属	戊	已
spleen	ministry	's	palace	section	Wu stem	follows

Zhōng	Yǒu	Míng	Tóng	Huáng	Cháng	Lǐ
中	有	明	童	黄	裳	里。
middle	exist	bright	boy	yellow	cloth	lining

Xiāo	Gǔ	Sàn	Qì	Shè	Yá	Chǐ
消	谷	散	气	摄	牙	齿
consume	grain	distribute	Qi	absorb	teeth	

Shì	Wéi	Tài	Cāng	Liǎng	Míng	Tóng
是	为	太	仓	两	明	童。
is	for	Great	Granary	two	bright	boy

Zuò	Zài	Jīn	Tái	Chéng	Jiǔ	Zhòng
坐	在	金	台	城	九	重
sit	at	golden	stage	city	nine-fold	

Fāng	Yuán	Yī	Cùn	Mìng	Mén	Zhōng
方	圆	一	寸	命	门	中。
circumference	one	inch	Life	Gate	within	

Chapter 2.13

The part of the palace dedicated to the Spleen comes from yang earth.[1]

In the middle, there is a bright boy wearing yellow clothes.

He controls the consummation of food and distribution of Qi, helping the absorption of nutrients.

In a Supreme Granary,[2] two bright boys are at work.

They sit at the golden stage of nine layers

in the one-inch circle around Ming-Men.

---

1) "Wu," heavenly stem, is a yang-earth phase (see the Glossary for the description of heavenly stems and earthly branches).

2) Acupuncture point Tai Cang: CV 12, associated with stomach function, which is represented here as a spiral flow, driven by two powers, feeding the Gate of Life.

Zhǔ	Diào	Bǎi	Gǔ	Wǔ	Wèi	Xiāng
主	调	百	谷	五	味	香
mainly	adjust	hundreds	grain	five	flavor	fragrance

Bì	Què	Xū	Yíng	Wú	Bìng	Shāng
辟	却	虚	赢	无	病	伤。
break	repulse	deficiency	extra	no	illness	injury

Wài	Yìng	Chǐ	Zhái	Qì	Sè	Fāng
外	应	尺	宅	气	色	芳

externally correspond (a unit of length) house complexion good

Guāng	Huá	Suǒ	Shēng	Yǐ	Biǎo	Míng
光	华	所	生	以	表	明。

brightness splendor therefore born by means of example

Huáng	Jǐn	Yù	Yī	Dài	Hǔ	Zhāng
黄	锦	玉	衣	带	虎	章
yellow	brocade	jade	robe	wear	tiger	seal

Zhù	Niàn	Sān	Lǎo	Zǐ	Qīng	Xiáng
注	念	三	老	子	轻	翔
	meditate	three	senior	self	light	fly

Chāng	Shēng	Gāo	Xiān	Yuǎn	Sǐ	Yāng
长	生	高	仙	远	死	殃。
long	life	high	immortal	far	death	calamity

Adjusting the hundred grains and five flavors.[1]

Break out from deficiency to prevent illness and injury

and externally radiate a great complexion.

Brightness induces splendor by means of example.

The robe of yellow brocade[2] with jade ornaments has the mark of a tiger.

Meditate on three old wizards gently soaring,[5]

rising high to the realm of the immortals, far from death and calamities.

---

3) The role of the spleen, according to Taoist teachings and TCM, is to extract the essence of the mixed "juice" of the ingested food, as five "flavors" (functions) that are distributed to the five Zang organs.

4) Yellow is the color of the Earth element (associated with Spleen).

5) Internal manifestations of the emperors of the Three Purities preside over the three Dan Tian. Soaring in heaven with them, or following a pattern of their accomplishment, indicates a return path of inner alchemy, re-integration to the primordial, Divine Origin (see Figure 4).

胆 部 章 第 十 四
Dǎn Bù Zhāng Dì Shí Sì
Gallbladder Section Chapter No. Fourteen

胆 部 之 宫 六 府 精
Dǎn Bù Zhī Gōng Liù Fǔ Jīng
gallbladder section 's palace six estate essence

中 有 童 子 曜 威 明。
Zhōng Yǒu Tóng Zǐ Yào Wēi Míng
middle there is virgin boy shine mighty brightness

雷 电 八 震 扬 玉 旌
Léi Diàn Bā Zhèn Yáng Yù Jīng
thunder lightning eight quakes spread jade banner

龙 旗 横 天 掷 火 铃。
Lóng Qí Héng Tiān Zhì Huǒ Líng
dragon flag horizontal sky throw fire bell

主 诸 气 力 摄 虎 兵
Zhǔ Zhū Qì Lì Shè Hǔ Bīng
mainly all Qi power absorb tiger soldier

外 应 眼 童 鼻 柱 间。
Wài Yìng Yǎn Tóng Bí Zhù Jiān
externally match eye pupil nose pillar between

脑 发 相 扶 亦 俱 鲜
Nǎo Fā Xiāng Fú Yì Jù Xiān
brain hair mutually nourish too altogether fresh

162

Chapter 2.14

The gall bladder's section of the palace has six parts of essence.[1]

In the middle, there is a virgin boy shining with mighty brightness

inducing eight waves of jade essence[2] with thunder and lighting.

A dragon flag across the sky plane radiates the energy of a ringing fire bell,[3]

passing central power to the tiger solders.

The office of Gall Bladder externally corresponds to the area between root of the nose and the eyes.

Brain and hair are mutually supported and bring freshness to the body.[4]

---

1) Gall Bladder exhibits the nature of all six Fu organs. It is a special case, because it is hollow like other Fu organs but stores a bile like Zang organs (bile molecules support the Fu transfer function by breaking down fat to help its digestion by body enzymes).

2) Continuity spreads through the eight aspects of change.

3) The Gall Bladder is visualized as a Fire Bell. Bile molecules, stored in Gall Bladder, are like soldiers that help break down fat. Energetically, the Gall Bladder also helps courage and righteous actions.

4) External and internal spirit support each other.

九 色 锦 衣 绿 华 裙。
Jiǔ Sè Jīn Yī Lǜ Huá Qún
nine color brocade clothes green magnificent gown

佩 金 带 玉 龙 虎 文
Pèi Jīn Dài Yù Lóng Hǔ Wén
wear gold with jade dragon tiger stripe

能 存 威 明 乘 庆 云
Néng Cún Wēi Míng Chéng Qìng Yún
able preserve mighty bright ride celebrate cloud

役 使 万 神 朝 三 元。
Yì Shǐ Wàn Shén Zhāo Sān Yuán
control tens of thousands spirits worship three Origins

The boy is clothed into green robe made of nine-colored brocade,

with gold and jade, dragon and tiger stripes,

That helps one survive a mighty ride on high clouds.

Gathering tens of thousands of sprits into worship of the three origins.[5]

---

5) The Three Purities, manifested in Heaven (1), Earth (2), and Man (3).

脾 长 章 第 十 五

Pí — Cháng — Zhāng — Dì — Shí — Wǔ

Spleen — chief — Chapter — No. Fifteen

脾	长	一	尺	掩	太	仓
Pí	Cháng	Yī	Chǐ	Yǎn	Tài	Cāng
spleen	length	one	foot	cover	Great	Granary

中	部	老	君	治	明	堂。
Zhōng	Bù	Lǎo	Jūn	Zhì	Míng	Táng
middle	section	senior	gentleman	rule	Light	Hall

厥	字	灵	元	名	混	康
Jué	Zì	Líng	Yuán	Míng	Hùn	Kāng
its	style name	spirit	primordial	name	drifting	air

治	人	百	病	消	谷	粮。
Zhì	Rén	Bǎi	Bìng	Xiāo	Gǔ	Liáng
treat	people	hundred	disease	digest	grain	food

黄	衣	紫	带	龙	虎	章
Huáng	Yī	Zǐ	Dài	Lóng	Hǔ	Zhāng
yellow	clothes	purple	scarf	dragon	tiger	seal

长	精	益	命	赖	君	王。
Cháng	Jīng	Yì	Mìng	Lài	Jūn	Wáng
increase	essence	benefit	life	depend on	sovereign	rule

三	呼	我	名	神	自	通
Sān	Hū	Wǒ	Míng	Shén	Zì	Tōng
three	call	my	name	spirit	naturally	understand

Chapter 2.15

The Spleen of one foot length covers a Great Storehouse.

In the middle section, Master Lao[1] rules the Hall of Brightness.

His pseudonym is Primordial Spirit, his name is Drifting in Peace.

To treat the hundred diseases, he manages transformation of the grain food.

He wears yellow clothes and a purple scarf with dragon and tiger seal

that catalyze Jing increase, and brings the abundance of life under the sovereign rule.

Through the triple calling of one's name, Spirit naturally reconnects to itself.

---

1) A pseudonym of Lao Zi (Most Exalted Lord Lao), who represents the Totality Centering (as Spleen is center of the 5 Zang organs and Earth is center of 5 elements) and a principle of re-integration in Alchemy (which is half-Divine, half-human discipline).

Sān	Lǎo	Tóng	Zuò	Gè	Yǒu	Péng
三	老	同	坐	各	有	朋。
three	senior	altogether	sit	each	has	friends
Huò	Jīng	Huò	Tāi	Bié	Zhí	Fāng
或	精	或	胎	别	执	方
either	Jing	or	fetus	separate	grasp	direction
Táo	Hái	Hé	Yán	Shēng	Huá	Máng
桃	孩	合	延	生	华	芒。
peach	child	fit	enhance	birth	brilliancy	
Nán	Nǚ	Huí	Jiǔ	Yǒu	Táo	Kāng
男	女	回	九	有	桃	康
male	female	return	nine	generate	peach	abundance
Dào	Fù	Dào	Mǔ	Duì	Xiāng	Wàng
道	父	道	母	对	相	望。
Tao	father	Tao	mother	face	each	other
Shī	Fù	Shī	Mǔ	Dān	Xuán	Xiāng
师	父	师	母	丹	玄	乡
master	master's	master	wife	pellet	mysterious	location
Kě	Yòng	Cún	Sī	Dēng	Xū	Kōng
可	用	存	思	登	虚	空。
can	use	store	thought	ascend	void	air
Shū	Tú	Yī	Huì	Guī	Yào	Zōng
殊	途	一	会	归	要	宗
unique	way	one	moment	return	must	end

Three seniors, placed alike, bring forth their friends.[2]

Jing and fetus grasp to separate directions.

Peach Child,[3] who is fit for enhancement, generates brilliancy.

The combination of nine distant male and female return paths forms the Peach of the Abundance.

Tao Father and Tao Mother face each other

as Male and Female Teacher, who form the elixir in a mysterious location

through deposit of their considerations to enable ascension into the void.[4]

The path of uniqueness must end to enable the path of return.

---

2) The three Dan Tian structure replicates throughout the body.

3) The peach is an ancient Taoist symbol of immortality.

4) This is the process of merging the established individual powers back to the void (TCs symmetry in Formula [1]). As unbalanced existence of a Being is a subject to dissipation, and Individual needs to integrate it with the personal Non-Being (back into Primordial Existence) upon completion of every manifestation cycle.

Bì	Sāi	Sān	Guān	Wò	Gù	Tíng
闭	塞	三	关	握	固	停。
close	squeeze	three	crossover	hold	hard	stop

Hán	Shù	Jīn	Lǐ	Tūn	Yù	Yīng
含	漱	金	醴	吞	玉	英。
keep	rinsing	gold	wine	swallow	jade	courage

Suì	Zhì	Bù	Jī	Sān	Chóng	Wáng
遂	致	不	饥	三	虫	亡。
succeed	reach	no	hunger	three	worms	perish

Xīn	Yì	Cháng	Hé	Zhì	Xīn	Chāng
心	意	常	和	致	欣	昌
regard		always	union	devote	happiness	prosperity

Wǔ	Yuè	Zhī	Yún	Qì	Péng	Hēng
五	岳	之	云	气	彭	亨。
five	mountain	's	cloud	Qi	expand	smooth

Bǎo	Guàn	Yù	Lú	Yǐ	Zì	Cháng
保	灌	玉	庐	以	自	偿
guard	irrigation	jade	hut	to	oneself	compensate

Wǔ	Xíng	Wán	Jiān	Wú	Zāi	Yāng
五	形	完	坚	无	灾	殃。
five	phases	to complete	strong	without		disaster

Close and contract three gateway points to cause firm stop.

Keep rinsing golden wine and swallow jade courage.[6]

Persevere until there is no hunger and the three worms will perish.[7]

Intend from kindness always, and this will bring happiness and prosperity.

The mist Qi from five mountains[8] will disperse smoothly.

Guard the jade hut of irrigation to compensate for personal manifestation.[9]

The five phases need to be completed fully to avoid leaks.

---

5) Oneness – Uniqueness – Individuality variants of One.

6) The flow through the five phases passes through and cannot be held, only its unsubstantial reflection, remaining in the center (peace, assurance/bravery of the accomplished) can be kept for good. This is similar to the concept in the Bhagavad Gita: "Who eats only a reminder of the sacrificial meal, will acquire no sin."

7) The three worms, or potentials for attachment, which by Taoist teachings nest at birth at person's head, chest, and genitals (and consume three treasures during life and after death) are: egoism, greed, and debauchery. They can feed through cracks at crossover points.

8) Five organs, or five elements, with respective functions. "Smoothness" associates images of polished jade and continuity to the intuitive mind of the practitioner and "smoothness of function," in the mathematic sense, to the analytical side of the mind (a function that has derivatives [see the Introduction], of all orders).

9) True individual existence (as Zhen Ren) is formed through a feeling of transcendence between rotations of Dan Tian and one's bodily manifestation and actions

上 睹 章 第 十 六
Shàng Dǔ Zhāng Dì Shí Liù
Supreme view Chapter No. Sixteen

上 睹 三 元 如 连 珠
Shàng Dǔ Sān Yuán Rú Lián Zhū
supreme view three origins as string of pearls

落 落 明 景 照 九 隅。
Luò Luò Míng Jǐng Zhào Jiǔ Yú
set down bright view shine nine corners

五 灵 夜 烛 焕 八 区
Wǔ Líng Yè Zhú Huàn Bā Qū
five spirits night illuminate brilliant eight areas

子 存 内 皇 与 我 游。
Zǐ Cún Nèi Huáng Yǔ Wǒ Yóu
child keep within emperor together I walk

身 披 凤 衣 衔 虎 符
Shēn Pī Fèng Yī Xián Hǔ Fú
body dressed phoenix dress hold tiger seal

一 至 不 久 升 虚 无。
Yī Zhì Bù Jiǔ Shēng Xū Wú
one arrive soon after ascend nothingness

Chapter 2.16

From the top view, three origins appear as a string of pearls.

Upon settling the bright view, it shins to nine corners.

The night of five spirits is illuminated by the brilliance of eight divisions.

The child emerging within the emperor makes it possible for Individuality to further,[1]

clothed in a dress of a phoenix to with the seal of the tiger.[2]

Oneness arrives soon after promoting nothingness.

---

1) Again, the alchemical process of "O-U-I Transformation" of the Identity-Centering aspect of IE symmetry. BTW, the insight of this principle seems to have been present in the organization of the Three Musketeers, described in writing of Alexander Dumas, through the famous attitude "All for One and One for All."

2) The elementary cycle of the day, where the grounding and synthetic principle of the Tiger (at the West) is assumed, after the peak of diversity in the rejuvenated flame of the Phoenix (at the South). Void and light are in the constant interplay which continues afterwards at North (Tortoise) and East (Dragon).

方寸之中念深藏
不方不圆闭牖窗。
三神还精老方壮
魂魄内守不争竞。
神生腹中衔玉当
灵注幽阙那得丧。
琳条万寻可荫仗
三魂既宁帝书命

A square inch inside a profound repository.[3]

Neither a square nor a round shutter can close the window of enlightenment.

The three spirits returning the essence of old, stir the new strength.[4]

Heavenly and Earthly spirit join in the continually developing perfection.[5]

The jade ornament carried in the middle of the abdomen withstands[6]

departure to seclusion and the ordinary death experience,

hiding strips of 10,000 gems in the shade, out of war zone.

The three immortal spirits in self-peace enter the Emperor's book of life.[7]

---

3) Personal experience integrated with the Universal (Collective) Truth.

4) The return of the completion (at the end of TCm transformation) to the void (via TCs transformation) brings the practitioner back to the origin, the new vitality of the Tao,

5) It is a paradoxal Truth than only the perfection (Earth) achieved at a specific level can serve as a base for further cultivation (Heaven).

6) Jade indicates Primordial Reality (synthesis of the polarities), that is formed, at the path of the return, in Lower Dan Tian.

7) A completed cycle of Three Purities (Formula [1]), writes dowen our ("Jade Writing") page in the Book of Life, as Manifestation of the Virtue, achieves the Merit in the Great Void.

灵 台 章 第 十 七
Líng Tái Zhāng Dì Shí Qī
Intelligence stand Chapter No. Seventeen

灵	台	郁	蔼	望	黄	野,
Líng	Tái	Yù	Ǎi	Wàng	Huáng	Yě
spirit	stand	fragrant	friendly	looking	yellow	field

三	寸	异	室	有	上	下。
Sān	Cùn	Yì	Shì	Yǒu	Shàng	Xià
three	inch	separate	room	have	top	bottom

间	关	营	卫	高	玄	受
Jiān	Guān	Yíng	Wèi	Gāo	Xuán	Shòu
space	pass	army	defend	high	mysterious	cultivation

洞	房	紫	极	灵	门	户。
Dòng	Fáng	Zǐ	Jí	Líng	Mén	Hù
inner	room	purple	pole	spirit		portal

是	昔	太	上	告	我	者
Shì	Xī	Tài	Shàng	Gào	Wǒ	Zhě
be	former	great	high	tell	I	person

左	神	公	子	发	神	语。
Zuǒ	Shén	Gōng	Zǐ	Fā	Shén	Yǔ
left	spirit	high	son	show	spirit	speech

176

Chapter 2.17

Spirit stands elegant and friendly as a full moon above the yellow plain.[1]

Three inches of space separate above from below.

A space made to defend high, mystical cultivation.

In a secret purple room, there is a portal of a high spirit.

Reflecting former high virtue of the Individuality.

Left spirit, high descendent, develops divine speech.

---

1) See Figure 4 (vertical axis), Individuality (Spirit) rises from the Plane of Manifestation of Oneness and Uniqueness (internally Qi and Jing)

Yòu	Yǒu	Bái	Yuán	Bìng	Lì	Chǔ
右	有	白	元	并	立	处
right	exist	white	origin	side by side	set up	office

Míng	Táng	Jīn	Kuì	Yù	Fáng	Jiān
明	堂	金	匮	玉	房	间。
bright	hall	gold	plated	jade		room

Shàng	Qīng	Zhēn	Rén	Dāng	Wú	Qián
上	清	真	人	当	吾	前
supreme	clarity	true	man	match	my	manifestation

Huáng	Cháng	Zǐ	Dān	Qì	Pín	Fán
黄	裳	子	丹	气	频	烦。
yellow	clothes	child	cinnabar	Qi	frequency	interference

Jiè	Wèn	Hé	Zài	Liǎng	Méi	Duān
借	问	何	在	两	眉	端
borrow	inquiry	where		both	eyebrows	

Nèi	Xiá	Rì	Yuè	Liè	Sù	Chén
内	侠	日	月	列	宿	陈
inside	knight	sun	moon	arrange	lodge	explain

Qī	Yào	Jiǔ	Yuán	Guān	Shēng	Mén
七	曜	九	元	冠	生	门。
seven	glorious	nine	origin	crown	birth	gate

178

On the right, side by side, there is a white primordial office,[2]

a hall of understanding, a gold-plated jade room.

Within supreme clarity stands a True Man, a manifestation of Individuality.

A boy in yellow clothes comes from Qi elixir made of interference of different frequencies,[3]

searches for an answer where both eyebrows meet.

The inner knight explains the mystery,[4] by the proper arrangement of sun and moon,

at the birth gate of seven glories and nine crowns of origin.

---

2) Traditional positions of three Taoist divinities are: Yuan Shi in the center, Ling Bao on the right, and Dao De (Lao Zi) on the left. The personal spirits of the same nature manifest in the body.

3) New, rejuvenated energy is born as a new combination resolved mysteries and difficulties (as dualities of the Supreme Purity).

4) The original True Man has a child aspect (entry into Mystery, via TCm symmetry of Formula [1]) and the knight aspect (one who resolves it by connecting all dots, on the return path (TCs symmetry of [1]).

三　关　章　第　十　八
Sān　Guān　Zhāng　Dì　Shí　Bā

Three　Passes　Chapter　No.　Eighteen

三　关　之　中　精　气　深
Sān　Guān　Zhī　Zhōng　Jìng　Qì　Shēn

three　junction　inside　essence　Qi　deep

九　微　之　内　幽　且　阴。
Jiǔ　Wēi　Zhī　Nèi　Yōu　Qiě　Yīn

nine　small　's　inside　secluded　further　Yin

口　为　心　关　精　神　机
Kǒu　Wéi　Xīn　Guān　Jìng　Shén　Jī

mouth　act　mind　junction　essence　spirit　engine

手　为　人　关　把　盛　衰
Shǒu　Wéi　Rén　Guān　Bǎ　Shèng　Shuāi

hand　act　man　junction　handle　rise and fall

足　为　地　关　生　命　哭。
Zú　Wéi　Dì　Guān　Shēng　Mìng　Kū

foot　act　Earth　junction　grow　life　cry

Chapter 2.18

There are three internal distinctions: Jing, Qi, and Shen.[1]

Nine profound internal chambers are secluded and most Yin.

The mouth acts as the central gateway of the vitality hub.

The hands act as gateways for man to hold the rise and fall.[2]

The feet act as the gateway to Earth, passing vitality and sickness.

---

1) A common translation of these would be essence, vitality, and spirit, but the Chinese words carry more internal meaning than that.

2) Each gateway interfaces two aspects of manifestation with one internal principle (in the form of TC symmetry). The important thing here is not the rise or fall by itself, but the know-how obtained as the result of balancing the pairs of opposites.

若 得 章 第 十 九
Ruǒ Dé Zhāng Dì Shí Jiǔ
If　Obtain　Chapter　No. Nineteen

若　得　三　宮　存　玄　丹
Ruǒ　Dé　Sān　Gōng　Cún　Xuán　Dān
if　obtain　three　palace　store　mysterious　elixir

太　一　流　珠　安　昆　仑。
Tài　Yī　Liú　Zhū　Ān　Kūn　Lún
great　one　floating　pearl　calm　Kunlun Mtn.

重　重　楼　阁　十　二　环
Zhòng　Zhòng　Lóu　Gé　Shí　Èr　Huán
one upon other　building　pavilion　twelve　stories

自　高　至　下　皆　真　人。
Zì　Gāo　Zhì　Xià　Jiē　Zhēn　Rén
from　above　to　below　each　True Man

玉　堂　绛　宇　尽　玄　宫
Yù　Táng　Jiàng　Yǔ　Jìn　Xuán　Gōng
jade　hall　red　space　throughout　mysterious　palace

璇　玑　玉　衡　色　兰　开。
Xuán　Jī　Yù　Héng　Sè　Lán　Kāi
jade　pearl　Jade Measure　appears　orchid　open

瞻　望　童　子　坐　盘　桓
Zhān　Wàng　Tóng　Zǐ　Zuò　Pán　Huán
gaze　to see　virgin　boy　sit　build　forever

Chapter 2.19

When you secure three palaces, store the mysterious elixir.

In highest stage, the elixir is like a floating pearl on the peaceful Kunlun Mountain.

The throat[1] is like a pagoda of 12 stories.

In each one (from top to bottom) resides a True Man.

In the red jade space,[2] throughout the mysterious palace

the pearl of Jade Measure (5th star of the Big Dipper) opens as a splendid orchid.

Gaze within to see a boy[3] sitting in divine play.

---

1) According to the "Internal Alchemy Pathways" picture shown in the on Figure 11, the throat is like a pagoda of 12 stories.

2) Indicates the heart area.

3) The Divine Boy Alchemist or "Stonecutter" who sends the gold pieces from the center of the heart to Heaven, the Big Dipper constellation.
The three palaces mentioned here are related to three upper archetypes on the Figure 11 (Alchemist Boy in Heart, Praying Monk in Throat and the Tao Master in Third Eye). They do not have any tools or associates as opposed the three Archetypes below (Weaving Lady, Cowherd and Water Pumping couple) and so they are part of the Return Path (self-formation) versus the Manifestation path (where Individuality is geared by environment provided helpers).

Wèn	Shuí	Jiā	Zǐ	Zài	Wǒ	Shēn。
问	谁	家	子	在	我	身。
ask	who	home	boy	exist	self	body

Cǐ	Rén	Hé	Qù	Rù	Ní	Wán
此	人	何	去	入	泥	丸
this	person	what	moved	enter	mud	ball

Qiān	Qiān	Bǎi	Bǎi	Zì	Xiāng	Lián。
千	千	百	百	自	相	连。
thousands		hundreds		oneself	mutual	connect

Yī	Yī	Shí	Shí	Sì	Zhòng	Shān
一	一	十	十	似	重	山
one	one	ten	ten	resemble	iteration	mountain

Yún	Yí	Yù	Huá	Xiá	Ěr	Mén。
云	仪	玉	华	侠	耳	门。
cloud	appearance	jade	splendid	knight	handles	gate

Chì	Dì	Kāi	Lǎo	Yǔ	Jǐ	Hún
赤	帝	开	老	与	己	魂
red	emperor	open	old	give	self	spirit

Sān	Zhēn	Fú	Xū	Gòng	Fáng	Jīn。
三	真	扶	胥	共	房	津。
three	true	support	assist	common	room	passage

Wǔ	Dǒu	Huàn	Míng	Shì	Qī	Yuán
五	斗	焕	明	是	七	元
five	Dipper	brilliant	understand	is	seven	origin

Asking who is the boy acting in a practitioner's body

and how it is related to the man within the brain.

There are hundreds of thousands of mutual links between them.

Each one separate or group together, they resemble the mountain chains.[4]

In a cloud at the top, a splendid jade knight handles the gate

of the Red Emperor, that opens towards the old Individuality spirit.

Three true supporters assist passage to a common area, along with

five Big Dipper constellation positions, each holding seven brilliant stars.[5]

---

4) The simpler ideas (e.g. archetypes of basis 1 or 10) are the foundation for more complex ones (hundreds, thousands). The relationship between the body and mind is like that between one and zero; the line of understanding is toward simplification, the line of action toward complexity. The Undefined variable (cloud) is the basis for both.

5) Five key points of time (inflexion points of periodic function), mapped to five positions of the Big Dipper constellation during the year (planetary evolution), are the basis for the manifestation of seven points of space (center, above, below, and four sides).

日 月 飞 行 六 合 间。

sun moon fly path six directions between

帝 乡 天 中 地 户 端

emperor village sky middle Earth household carry

面 部 魂 神 皆 相 存。

face ministry liver heart spirit each mutually store

Sun and moon are related through six paths.

The emperor village is in the middle of the sky, suspending the Earth and the household below.[6]

The face and soul mirror and preserve each other.[7]

---

6) A point of existence in the present time is a "carrier" of personal space toward any direction. The primordial existence (Sun) is related to temporal existence (Moon) through six lines of "Yi Jing", the six archetypes on Figure 11 or six transformations in the TC symmetry, in Formula [1].

7) A manifested "time circle" (which defines passage from motionless to motion and vice versa) mirrors the "phase space circle" (in which unsubstantial transmutes to substantial and vice versa), as the Moon mirrors the Sun.

呼 吸 章 第 二 十

Breathe Out/In   Chapter   No. Twenty

呼 吸 元 气 以 求 仙

breathe   original   Qi   in order to seek   immortality

仙 公 公 子 已 在 前。

immortal   grandfather   son   then   going   forward.

朱 鸟 吐 缩 白 石 源

red   bird   emerges   withdraws   snowy   rock   origin

结 精 育 胞 化 生 身。

produce   essence   raise   womb   change   birth   body

留 胎 止 精 可 长 生

preserve   fetus   stop   essence   enable   eternal   living

三 气 右 回 九 道 明。

three   Qi   right   revolve   nine   Tao   lights

188

Chapter 2.20

Breathe original (Yuan) Qi in order to become Immortal.

When the grandfather achieves immortality, the son can go on.[1]

The red bird emerges and withdraws from its nest within snowy rocks.[2]

When essence is plentiful the womb area would ascend.[3]

Guard the fetus and stop the essence generation to support living in eternity.

Three Qi should be revolved clockwise nine times to see the Tao light.

---

1) One generation represents a cultivation cycle (manifestation or sublimation), two generations indicate a full period (TC transformation) of completeness (see Formula [1]). When the accomplishment of the full dual cycle is settled without inner contradictions (grandfather), the new cycle (son) can start.

2) The red bird relates to the tongue, rocks to the teeth. A referenced form of cleansing consists of expelling non-integrated Post-Heaven Qi along the tongue during exhalation.

3) The steam of essence rises through all bones and finally nourishes the brain. When the essence originated in the lower Dan Tian (womb of Jing) saturates the body, it transforms to Qi, sourced in middle Dan Tian (the womb of Qi).

Zhèng	Yī	Hán	Huá	Nǎi	Chōng	Yíng
正	一	含	华	乃	充	盈
straight	one	keep	splendid	to be	abundant	

Yáo	Wàng	Yī	Xīn	Rú	Luó	Xīng
遥	望	一	心	如	罗	星。
look	distance	one	heart	as if	catch	star

Jīn	Shì	Zhī	Xià	Kě	Bù	Qīng
金	室	之	下	可	不	倾
gold	room	's	floor	can	not	collapse

Yán	Wǒ	Bái	Shǒu	Fǎn	Hái	Yīng
延	我	白	首	反	孩	婴。
extend	self	white	chief	reverse	child	infant

The vertical axis collects splendor to enable abundance.

Look to the distance with an integrated mind and body as if you want to catch a star.

A room with the gold floor can not collapse[4].

Extend oneself through the white chief reversing to infant child.

---

4) If Qi and Jing are plentiful (in lower two Dan Tians), Shen can soar exploring the mystery (from Upper Dan Tian).

琼 室 章 第 二 十 一

Jasper Room   **Chapter**   **No. Twenty One**

Qióng	Shì	Zhī	Zhōng	Bā	Sù	Jí
琼	室	之	中	八	素	集
jasper	room	's	inside	eight	silk	collections

Ní	Wán	Fū	Rén	Dāng	Zhōng	Lì
泥	丸	夫	人	当	中	立。
mud	pill	madam		in the center		stand

Cháng	Gǔ	Xuán	Xiāng	Rào	Xiào	Yì
长	谷	玄	乡	绕	效	邑
eternal	valley	mysterious	village	rotate	replicate	city

Liù	Lóng	Sàn	Fēi	Nán	Fēn	Bié
六	龙	散	飞	难	分	别。
six	dragon	discharge	flight	difficulty	to part	

Cháng	Shēng	Zhì	Shèn	Fáng	Zhōng	Jí
长	生	至	慎	房	中	急
long life		very	careful	house	central	urgent

Hé	Wéi	Sǐ	Zuò	Líng	Shén	Qì
何	为	死	作	令	神	泣。
how	to pass	un-crossable	to do	order	spirit	to sob

Hū	Zhī	Huò	Xiāng	Sān	Líng	Mò
忽	之	祸	乡	三	灵	殁
overlook	it	disaster	village	three	spirit	die

Chapter 2.21

The jade room has eight silk repositories inside.

The mud ball lady stands in the center.[1]

The eternal valley around which the mysterious village rotates, to replicate the city.[2]

Six dragons dispense the flow of difficulties to base elements.[3]

Long life comes to those who are extremely cautious about the desires of the central house.[4]

Passing across the un-crossable border causes the spirit to sob.

Neglecting this causes disaster to the village and the death of three spirits.

---

1) The brain has nine sections; the mud ball (ni-wan) is the central one.

2) Processing of ideas within the brain goes through eight trigrams, in a full symmetry cycle, replicating a divine template.

3) The Six Fu organs transform substances and clear impurities.

4) Do not let the essence drain out through lustful behavior or thoughts, as that would exhaust the triple principle of reintegration (see Figure 4).

Dàn 但 but	Dāng 当 persist	Xī 吸 absorb	Qì 气 Qi	Lù 录 replicate	Zǐ 子 child	Jīng 精。 essence
Cùn 寸 inch	Tián 田 field	Chǐ 尺 foot	Zhái 宅 residence	Kě 可 can	Zhì 治 induce	Shēng 生 rebirth
Ruò 若 if	Dāng 当 persist	Jué 决 determine	Hǎi 海 sea	Bǎi 百 hundred	Dú 渎 trouble	Qīng 倾。 overturn
Yè 叶 leaves	Qù 去 go	Shù 树 tree	Kū 枯 dry	Shī 失 lose	Qīng 青	Qīng 青、 green color
Qì 气 Qi	Wáng 亡 perish	Yè 液 fluid	Lòu 漏 leak	Fēi 非 not	Jǐ 己 oneself	Xíng 形。 form
Zhuān 专 focus	Bì 闭 shut	Yù 御 defend	Jǐng 景 circumstance	Nǎi 乃 then	Cháng 长 constant	Níng 宁 peace
Bǎo 保 defend	Wǒ 我 my	Ní 泥 mud	Wán 丸 ball	Sān 三 three	Qí 奇 wonderful	Líng 灵。 spirits
Tián 恬 contended	Dàn 淡	Bì 闭 shut	Shì 视 look	Nèi 内 inside	Zì 自 one's	Míng 明 brightness

However, persistently absorb Qi and plant a strong seed of essence.

The one-inch field within a one-foot estate, and be able to induce rebirth.

If one is able to persist, certainly the sea of 100 troubles will overturn.[5]

If leaves fall, the tree will wither, losing its fresh green color.

Qi would perish and fluids leak out, and one won't be able to rejuvenate.

Therefore, focus on the perimeter of defense, in order to preserve peace.

Defend own mud ball and three wonderful spirits.

Quiet and content, shut the eyes and observe internal brightness.

---

5) Continual accumulation and circulation of Qi along the descending flow without leak will ensure generation of the active Jing. Once Jing is full, the TC symmetry reversal (Ds crossover form Formula [1]) will ensure rejuvenation flow upwards, the Heavenly River would generate fresh Qi and enable the rebirth of Shen.

Wù	Wù	Bù	Gān	Tài	Ér	Píng
物	物	不	干	泰	而	平。
things		unwilling		grand	not	calm

Yì	Què	Fěi	Shì	Lǎo	Fù	Dīng
意	悫	匪	事	老	复	丁
desire	sincere	thief	affair	old	recover	shape

Sī	Yǒng	Yù	Shū	Rù	Shàng	Qīng
思	咏	玉	书	入	上	清。
think	sing	jade	book	enter	high	purity

Matters incompatible with greatness[6] will not calm down.

However, if the thieves of desire are abandoned, the old man should recover to a good shape.

Think or recite the text of this jade book internally and enter the highest purity.

---

6) Only Pre-Heaven Jing, Qi and Shen, which are in great harmony (subject to accomplished symmetries, as in Pre-Heaven Ba Gua), constitute the rejuvenated body of the Practitioner. The temporal patterns and selfish intent would need to be purged out.

Cháng	Niàn	Zhāng	Dì	Èr	Shí	Èr
常	念	章	第	二	十	二
Always	Study	Chapter		No.	Twenty	Two

Cháng	Niàn	Sān	Fáng	Xiāng	Tōng	Dá
常	念	三	房	相	通	达
always	study	three	room	mutual	open	achieve

Dòng	Shì	Dé	Jiàn	Wú	Nèi	Wài
洞	视	得	见	无	内	外。
void	look	suitable	see	neither	internal	external

Cún	Shù	Wǔ	Yá	Bù	Jī	Kě
存	漱	五	芽	不	饥	渴
store	rinse	five	sprout	not	hungry	thirsty

Shén	Huá	Zhí	Jīn	Liù	Dīng	Yè
神	华	执	巾	六	丁	谒。
spirit	splendid	grasp	cloth	six	shapes	visit

Jí	Shǒu	Jīng	Shì	Wù	Wàng	Xiè
急	守	精	室	勿	妄	泄
careful	guard	essence	room	do not	absurd	leak

Bì	Ér	Bǎo	Zhī	Kě	Cháng	Huó
闭	而	宝	之	可	长	活。
close	and	treasure	it	able	always	live

Qǐ	Zì	Xíng	Zhōng	Chū	Bù	Kuò
起	自	形	中	初	不	阔
rise	oneself	form	center	basic	not	rich

Chapter 2.22

Always study with the three rooms mutually connected.

The achieved void doesn't feel either external or internal[1].

Rinse and ingest five pearls, to avoid being hungry or thirsty.

The spirit grasps the brilliant cloth that passes through six bowls.[2]

Carefully guard essence; do not allow the room to leak in vain.

Adjust the complementing treasures so you can always live.[3]

Establish your form from the center, in the basic and not the complex way.

---

1) The Individual Non-Being and the space of personal potentials (Phase Space), symbolized by the Dragon, displayed on Figure 4.

2) Five Zang organs assimilate and store Yin essences. Six Fu organs are driven by a change pattern (cloth) to pass through and do not hold the flow.

3) Yin and Yang organs, balanced around Individual Void, supplement each other and enable the prosperous life.

Sān	Guān	Jìn	Zài	Yì	Yǐn	Kuò
三	官	近	在	易	隐	括。
three	organ	near	middle	exchange	hidden	enclosure

Xū	Wú	Jì	Jì	Kōng	Zhōng	Suǒ
虚	无	寂	寂	空	中	索
void	not have	solitary		air	middle	rope

Shǐ	Xíng	Rú	Shì	Bù	Dāng	Wū
使	形	如	是	不	当	污。
enable	form	as	to be	not	act	dirt

Jiǔ	Shì	Zhèng	Xū	Shén	Míng	Shè
九	室	正	虚	神	明	舍
nine	room	upright	void	spirit	bright	residence

Cún	Sī	Bǎi	Niàn	Shì	Jié	Dù
存	思	百	念	视	节	度。
keep	consider	hundred	study	observe	economy	measure

Liù	Fǔ	Xiū	Zhì	Wù	Lìng	Gù
六	府	修	治	勿	令	故
six	mansion	cultivate	govern	do not	cause	old

Xíng	Zì	Áo	Xiáng	Rù	Tiān	Lù
行	自	翱	翔	入	天	路。
go	oneself	soar	high	enter	Heavenly	road

Three offices near to the center form the hidden enclosure.[4]

Unengaged but not solitary, a tube of void is in the middle.[5]

This makes it possible for the body form not to get dirty.

The nine palaces above are clear and void, so brilliant spirit comes to stay.

Keep considered number of studies under control[6].

The six mansions[7] should be cultivated and governed to avoid aging.

Overcome yourself, soar high, and enter the Heavenly path.

---

4) The Lower Dan Tian is a center of the body, without any attributes. It indirectly joins the surrounding parameters of changes (three axis around the central point in Figure 2 or Figure 4), specifically synchronizes Yin and Yang Jing and Jing and Qi.

5) A virtue achieved by accomplished alchemy process, symbolized by Dragon on Figure 4.

6) The scoop of the finite cultivation cycle (base of the spiral on Figure 4) should target reasonably achievable set of new mysteries.

7) Six steps of the cultivation process, "Yi Jing" hexagram lines, illustrated in Formula [1] or six archetype activities on Figure 11.

治　生　章　第　二　十　三

Manage　Life　Chapter　No. Twenty Three

治　生　之　道　了　不　烦

manage　living　's　Tao　know　no　confusion

但　修　洞　玄　与　玉　篇。

only　cultivate　cave　mysterious　and　jade　sheet

兼　行　形　中　八　景　神

double　circulation　form　middle　eight　bright　spirit

二　十　四　真　出　自　然。

twenty four　truth　produce　oneself　Nature

高　拱　无　为　魂　魄　安

tall　arch　not　doing　Heaven Earth Spirit　peace

清　净　神　见　与　我　言。

clear　completely　spirit　see　with　own　words

Chapter 2.23

Manage the rebirth of the Tao without confusion.

Simply cultivate emptiness by studying the mysterious Jade Chapters.[1]

The double pass formation centers the eight bright spirits[2] within.

Twenty-four truths reproduce themselves naturally.[3]

The highest arch doesn't have to conform to either the Heaven or Earth spirit—it is at peace.[4]

Completely clear the Shen (spirit of the unique personality) and let it integrate with the spirit of Truth.

---

1) Yu Pian, Jade Chapters, was the Chinese dictionary from 543 C.E, containing over 12,000 different characters. A study of many of its symbols results in finding silent simplicity (similar to the study from multiple points of view/knowledge systems).

2) Two repetition of the periodic function in a standing wave inside (the sample change function on Figure 5, along with the reflection wave) the circulating Dan Tian have eight inflection (gradient changing) points.

3) The eight gradient changing points in all three (Upper, Middle, and Lower) Dan Tian yield twenty four. The Jing, Qi and Shen dimensions produce seventy two patterns, as presented on Feng Shui Compass on Figure 9.

4) The gradient of Dan Tian wave function extremes (at 90, 270 degrees, for both direct and reflection wave) is associated neither to the work of Heaven (descending gradient) nor Earth (ascending gradient). It is unchanging (gradient parallel to axis), enabling inner peace and merge with Tao.

Ān 安 calm	Zài 在 at	Zǐ 紫 purple	Fáng 房 room	Wéi 帏	Mù 幕 curtain	Jiān 间 separate
Lì 立 lay down	Zuò 坐 fruition	Shì 室 room	Wài 外 external	Sān 三 three	Wǔ 五 five	Xuán 玄。 mysteries
Shāo 烧 burn	Xiāng 香 incense	Jiē 接 receive	Shǒu 手 hand	Yù 玉 jade	Huá 华 splendid	Qián 前 front
Gòng 共 together	Rù 入 enter	Tài 太 highest	Shì 室 room	Xuán 璇 jade	Jī 玑 pearl	Mén 门。 gate
Gāo 高 high	Yán 研 study	Tián 恬	Dàn 淡 tranquil	Dào 道 Tao	Zhī 之 's	Yuán 园 garden
Nèi 内 internal	Shì 视 look	Mì 密 secret	Pàn 盼 hope	Jìn 尽 finally	Dǔ 睹 see	Zhēn 真。 Truth
Zhēn 真 True	Rén 人 Man	Zài 在 exist	Jǐ 己 oneself	Mò 莫 none	Wèn 问 ask	Lín 邻 close to
Hé 何 what	Chǔ 处 dwell	Yuǎn 远 distant	Suǒ 索 demand	Qiú 求 seek	Yīn 因 reason	Yuán 缘。 edge

They would calmly meet in a purple room with a curtain between them

and lay down the mysterious five-fold transformation of the three Dan Tian.[5]

Burn the incense of welcome to connect to a splendid jade in front of you.

Modestly enter the highest room through the gate of jade and pearl.

Meditate with the highest aspiration to enter the tranquil Tao garden.

Look internally with the highest solemnity, ready to see the true, objective reality.

True Man exists as an indivisible spirit—there is nothing to get attached to.

At the far edges of the view, the new aspects of the mystery seek to become a part of the destiny.

---

5) While the eight-fold change in the three Dan Tian represents a single plane cultivation cycle, the five-fold change represents the transcending cycle that would eventually emerge (fifth point at 360 degrees of specific period function representing a new version of the first point at 0 degrees).

6) Totality centering process is continuous and never-ending. Every break through (integration to a space of Truth) brings the practitioner into the world of the higher symmetries.

隐影章第二十四

Secret Appears Chapter No. Twenty Four

Yǐn	Xíng	Miè	Xíng	Yǔ	Shì	Shū
隐	形	灭	形	与	世	殊
secret	appear	drown	shape	give	life	unique

Hán	Qì	Yǎng	Jīng	Kǒu	Rú	Zhū
含	气	养	精	口	如	朱
keep	Qi	raise	essence	mouth	such	vermillion

Dài	Zhí	Xìng	Mìng	Shǒu	Xū	Wú
带	执	性	命	守	虚	无
raise	grasp	nature	life	guard	void	none

Míng	Rù	Shàng	Qīng	Sǐ	Lù	Chú
名	入	上	清	死	录	除
name	enter	high	purity	impassable	copy	remove

Sān	Shén	Zhī	Lè	Yóu	Yǐn	Jū
三	神	之	乐	由	隐	居。
three	spirit	's	laugh	from	secret	residence

Shū	Yàn	Yóu	Áo	Wú	Yí	Yōu
倏	焱	游	遨	无	遗	忧
sudden	spark	tour	travel	not have	lose	concern

Yǔ	Fú	Yī	Zhèng	Bā	Fēng	Qū
羽	服	一	正	八	风	驱。
feather	clothes	one	principle	eight	wind	drive

Chapter 2.24

The mystery that appears extinguished shapes into a new unique aspect of the practitioner's life.[1]

Maintain the raise of Qi from the essence below with the help of the phoenix within the mouth.[2]

Grasp the new life, but do not get attached to it, stay firmly in the void.[3]

When the new nature of the individual enters the high purity, the old (non-integrated) nature would be cleared.[4]

Three core spiritual aspects of Individuality stay happy in their secret residence,

not concerned by another sudden mystical excursion.[5]

Their feather clothes guide eight winds of a single intent,[6]

---

1) Uniqueness is the essence of life. The mystery that didn't become integrated into Individual Truth (perfection, Yang) in the previous cycle forms a "grain of sand in an oyster shell" (Yin, imperfection), a base of pearl (Zhen, Truth) of the next cycle.

2) The vermillion (red) bird or phoenix symbolizes the tongue. Tongue reaching the palate helps activation of Du vessel.

3) The cultivation cycle (transforming Jing to Qi and Qi to Shen) should be regulated from the "seat in peace", the center.,

4) Internal "software" (genetic and spiritual) would be upgraded.

5) Virtue (Te) achieved through the Unique work of the Individual for Oneness is incorruptible, always integrated with Tao.

6) Pre-Heaven Ba Gua (or the eight winds), established in Oneness through centering, is formed as the result of the Individual addressing the previous manifestation challenges.

控	驾	三	素	乘	晨	霞
Kòng	Jià	Sān	Sù	Chéng	Chén	Xiá
charge	harness	three	silk	ride	dawn	clouds

金	辇	正	立	从	玉	舆。
Jīn	Niǎn	Zhèng	Lì	Cóng	Yù	Yú
gold	carriage	upright	setup	from	jade	carriage

何	不	登	山	诵	我	书
Hé	Bù	Dēng	Shān	Sòng	Wǒ	Shū
what	no	ascend	mountain	read	individual	book

郁	郁	窈	窕	真	人	墟。
Yù	Yù	Yǎo	Tiǎo	Zhēn	Rén	Xū
elegant	quiet	secluded	true	man	rest	

入	山	何	难	故	踌	躇
Rù	Shān	Hé	Nán	Gù	Chóu	Chú
enter	mountain	what	difficult	cause	waver	hesitate

人	间	纷	纷	臭	如	如。
Rén	Jiān	Fēn	Fēn	Chòu	Rú	Rú
man	between	numerous		wave	handkerchief	such

and they ride colorful clouds controlled by a triple silk harness,[7]

in a golden carriage, made of jade components, going always toward higher good.[8]

What does not ascend the mountain, reading the book of Individualization

is a wonderful quiet seclusion place where True Man rests[9].

The mountain of new difficulty is entered when there is hesitation, pacing back and forth,

but new man is formed from the middle of the conflicts[10].

---

7) Silk reeling in Tai Chi represents various paths in re-integrating the Oneness. Three threads of the silk reeling indicate Being, Non-Being and the True Nature (Figure 1).

8) The asymmetry of constant cultivation in spirit, as opposed to an attachment to the pairs of contradictions of the manifested world.

9) The prosperity and advancement (movement) is complemented by the unchanging, immutable higher self, True Man within (peace).

10) Yin (symbolized in "Yi Jing" by the line broken in two) symbolizes an oscillation, symmetry of the two polarities. A hesitation of the Individual to achieve integration presents attachment to a Yin World and prevents ascend. Only the full integration which is Yang supports Individuality-preserving cross-over to the higher space. The path of integration is rooted in the conflicts, same as the lotus grows from mud (see Figure 1, which also represent Lotus palm hand gesture). Buddhists say that the root of suffering is also the root of liberation and the western magician Elifas Levi said that the Tree of Knowledge and the Tree of Life have the same root.

五 行 章 第 二 十 五

Wǔ Xíng Zhāng Dì Èr Shí Wǔ

Five Currents Chapter No. Twenty Five

五	行	相	推	反	归	一
Wǔ	Xíng	Xiāng	Tuī	Fǎn	Guī	Yī
five	currents	portrait	refuse	return	back	one

三	五	合	气	九	九	节。
Sān	Wǔ	Hé	Qì	Jiǔ	Jiǔ	Jié
three	five	join	Qi	nine times nine		segment

可	用	隐	地	回	八	术
Kě	Yòng	Yǐn	Dì	Huí	Bā	Shù
able	use	secret	ground	revolve	eight	method

伏	牛	幽	阙	罗	品	列。
Fú	Niú	Yōu	Què	Luó	Pǐn	Liè
hide	ox	secluded	post	gather	variety	row

三	明	出	华	生	死	际
Sān	Míng	Chū	Huá	Shēng	Sǐ	Jì
three	light	produce	splendid	life and death		boundary

洞	房	灵	象	斗	日	月。
Dòng	Fáng	Líng	Xiàng	Dǒu	Rì	Yuè
cave	room	spirit	form	Dipper	Sun	Moon

父	曰	泥	丸	母	雌	一
Fù	Yuē	Ní	Wán	Mǔ	Cí	Yī
father	speak	mud	ball	mother	female	one

210

Chapter 2.25

Five streams act upon each other and return to Oneness.

Three and five Qi join in the nine times nine field[1].

Staying on secret ground, one is able to perform the eightfold method revolution.[2]

Between buffalo horns hiding on a secluded port, the new variety forms.[3]

Triple radiance produces the splendid boundary of life or death.[4]

Spirit from the central cave originates new seasons of the Big Dipper revolution.

Yang aspect gathers in separate thinking of the head, Yin aspect in oneness of the body.

---

1) See the table on Figure 6.

2) One pre-Heaven field surrounded by eight new post Heaven fields

3) Water Buffalo horns represent Kidneys, like two poles of the magnet, that accumulate essence.

4) Establishing of the Dan Tian (center of body) as the border between manifestation and sublimation (TCm and TCs symmetries in Formula [1]), where the descending wave of formation reflects back (Figure 10). Leaks lead to dissipation, but return (flow streaming upwards) leads to re-integration.

Èr	Guāng	Huàn	Zhào	Rù	Zǐ	Shì
二	光	焕	照	入	子	室。
two	ray	brilliant	shine	enter	son	room

Néng	Cún	Xuán	Zhēn	Wàn	Shì	Bì
能	存	玄	真	万	事	毕
capable	store	mysterious	true	ten thousand	thing	completeness

Yī	Shēn	Jīng	Shén	Bù	Kě	Shī
一	身	精	神	不	可	失。
one	body	essence	spirit	not	able	lost

Two brilliant rays shine, entering the room of the son,[5]

making it possible to store the mysterious Truth of the centered view to 10,000 things.

In a body that is one with the whole world, the spirit of essence cannot be lost.

---

5)   New integration of mind and body (immortal fetus).

高 奔 章 第 二 十 六
High Rush Chapter — **No. Twenty Six**

高	奔	日	月	吾	上	道
high	towards	Sun	Moon	individual	higher	Tao

郁	仪	结	磷	善	相	保。
elegant	produce	luster	perfect	mutual	guarantee	

乃	见	玉	清	虚	无	老
thus	look	jade	clarity	void	without	old

可	以	回	颜	填	血	脑。
able	use	return	color	fill	fluid	brain

口	衔	灵	芒	携	五	皇
mouth	hold	spirit	awn	carry	five	emperor

腰	带	虎	录	佩	金	焱
waist	band	tiger	signs	wear	gold	ornament

驾	焱	接	生	宴	东	蒙。
harness	swift	receive	birth	feast	mountain	east

Chapter 2.26

The integration of the lights of Sun and Moon[1] enables a high individual Tao.

The graceful luster guarantees achievement of perfection.

Thus one can appear integral in the Jade Purity[2], without signs of age.

Colors generated through revolving work will fill the fluid of the brain.

The mouth holds the spirit sprouts embodying the five principles.[3]

Around the waist, wear a band with the golden symbol of the tiger.

Ride a swift dragon to enjoy the feast on the east mountain.

---

1) The integration of the reflected light of the higher archetypes (Moon light that one achieves during descending, on TCm path) and the internally generated light (Sun, on TCs path of re-integration, in Formula [1]) brings the practitioner to a central achievement, that balances the both paths.

2) The re-integration (TCs) path completes in the Jade Purity, the Primordial Wu Ji (as a completion of the sequence 1-2-3-3-2-1 mentioned in Introduction).

3) Governing principles of the five elements/Zang organs and five flavors.

玄元章第二十七

Xuán Yuán Zhāng Dì Èr Shí Qī

Mysterious Origin Chapter No. Twenty Seven

玄 元 上 一 魂 魄 炼
mysterious origin high one Heaven Earth spirit refine

一 之 为 物 叵 卒 见。
one 's to become matter not finish meet

须 得 至 真 乃 顾 盼
wait obtain arrive true thus attend expect

至 忌 死 气 诸 秽 贱。
arrive fear rigid Qi all dirt cheap

六 神 合 集 虚 中 宴
six spirit join gather void middle feast

结 珠 固 精 养 神 根。
produce pearl solid essence raise spirit root

玉 匙 金 龠 常 完 坚
jade keyhole gold key always entire strong

216

Chapter 2.27

The mysterious, highest origin of the united spirit of Heaven and Earth should be refined.[1]

This oneness appearing in substance is not complete.

Patiently wait until Truth is obtained; only then can you act.

To cultivate the primordial, one must keep Qi clear from all unclean and superficial attachments.

The six Fu spirits will join together in the Dan Tian void, like they come to a feast.

They will produce the pearl of solid essence for the spirit root to grow.[2]

The central achievement is made by unlocking jade keyhole by gold key and always stays strong[3].

---

1) Po is the spirit of lungs (metal element) determining attachment to the substantial. Hun is the spirit of liver (wood element), driving aspiration to non-substantial existence. See Figure 5 in the Introduction for associations of these two and three other elemental spirits.

2) Insubstantial structural patterns manifest substantial energy, similar to the way substantial events create insubstantial Truth (similar to Einstein's formulas of General Relativity, where geometry is balanced by matter).

3) Keyhole is the manifestation plane of essence and vitality, Jing and Qi, while the key is spirit, Shen (see the axis on Figure 4). Their interaction locks (via TCm symmetry) to the enfolded (substantial) manifestation and unlocks (via TCs symmetry). to the unfolded (insubstantial) Primordial existence.

Bì	Kǒu	Qū	Shé	Shí	Tāi	Jīn
闭	口	屈	舌	食	胎	津
close	mouth	bent	tongue	eat	elixir	saliva

Shǐ	Wǒ	Suì	Liàn	Huò	Fēi	Xiān
使	我	遂	炼	获	飞	仙。
make	individual	satisfy	refine	harvest	fly	immortal

Close the mouth, bend the tongue to the top palate, and drink the elixir[4] within the saliva.

Complete the process that refines Individuality and enjoy becoming a flying Immortal.

---

4) Also called "jade liquid," the solidifying energy pattern which is "encoded" into physical saliva.

仙人章第二十八
Xiān Rén Zhāng Dì Èr Shí Bā

Immortal Man **Chapter** **No. Twenty Eight**

仙 人 道 士 非 有 神
Xiān Rén Dào Shì Fēi Yǒu Shén
immortal man / Tao / scholar / not be / exist / spirit

积 精 累 气 以 为 真。
Jī Jīng Léi Qì Yǐ Wéi Zhēn
accumulate essence cumulate Qi in order to become truth

黄 童 妙 音 难 可 闻
Huáng Tóng Miào Yīn Nán Kě Wén
yellow child wonderful sound difficulty can fame

玉 书 绛 简 赤 丹 文。
Yù Shū Jiàng Jiǎn Chì Dān Wén
jade book purple simple red cinnabar writing

字 曰 真 人 巾 金 巾
Zì Yuē Zhēn Rén Jīn Jīn Jīn
word speak true man cloth gold cloth

负 甲 持 符 开 七 门。
Fù Jiǎ Chí Fú Kāi Qī Mén
lose shell persevere seal write seven gate

火 兵 符 图 备 灵 关
Huǒ Bīng Fú Tú Bèi Líng Guān
fire force seal diagram prepare spirit cross

Chapter 2.28

Immortals and Tao adepts do not aspire only to Spirit.[1]

They cultivate Essence and Qi in order to embody Truth.[2]

Children of the middle path learn to play difficult melodies, to achieve Virtue.

The Jade Writing is written in simple, but subtle, red and purple calligraphy.

Words spoken by True Men[3] are like a scarf of gold.

Their armors are sealed by inscriptions at the seven gates.[4]

The seals are made as diagrams by powers of fire, enabling the crossover only of the good spirits.

---

1) Unlike adepts from some other lines, Taoists do not forsake body cultivation, considering it as a part of existence.

2) Their goal is to find their own eternal Individuality in Truth and to follow the path of continuous cultivation (walk with God). They rigorously overcome themselves internally, while externally gently helping the peace and prosperity of the world.

3) Zhen Ren is initially an ordinary man, who achieved existence in Truth and became exempt from certain laws (symmetry systems) in Nature. This is similar to a principle through which the conscious beings raised themselves (vertically) above the animals (conforming to 2D, body symmetry and a perception focused on the own area of the planetary surface) and animals got higher freedom, comparing to plants focused to 1D growth.

4) The seven gates (see Figure 10) are: Heavenly gate (Tian Men) on the top of the head, Earth gate (Di Men) at tailbone, Middle gate (Zhong Men or Ming Men) at the lower back, Health gate (Feng Men) at the middle of back, Ascending gate (Hou Men) at the back of the head. Bridge gate (Qian Men) at the upper palate, and Building gate (Lou Men) at the solar plexus.

Qián	Áng	Hòu	Bēi	Gāo	Xià	Chén
前	昂	后	卑	高	下	陈。
first	raise	afterwards	low	high	down	lay out

Zhí	Jiàn	Bǎi	Zhàng	Wǔ	Jǐn	Fān
执	剑	百	丈	舞	锦	幡
grasp	sword	hundred	ten feet	dance	brocade	banner

Shí	Jué	Pán	Kōng	Shàn	Fēn	Yún
十	绝	盘	空	扇	纷	纭。
ten	vanish	tray	air	fan	disorder	confusion

Huǒ	Líng	Guān	Xiāo	Duì	Luò	Yān
火	铃	冠	霄	队	落	烟
fire	bell	crest	firmament	group	leave	mist

Ān	Zài	Huáng	Què	Liǎng	Méi	Jiān
安	在	黄	阙	两	眉	间
calm	exist	yellow	scarce	two	eyebrow	between

Cǐ	Fēi	Zhī	Yè	Shí	Shì	Gēn
此	非	枝	叶	实	是	根。
this	not be	branch	leaf	real	is	root

First rising then falling, in top-down swing,

by sword-fingers, through a rich, 10-foot dance, on a brocade banner.

Their power would vanquish all energy disorders knocking on the doors of the body.

In a sealed body, fire rises to the top of the head, mist drops down.[5]

Calmness settles in the imperial city between two eyebrows.

This is not a branch or leaf, but a true root.[6]

---

5) The waterwheel path in the body is similar to the circulation of water in nature. As water evaporates to clouds, then falls as rain, in the Microcosmic orbit of man, Qi raises from Dan Tian to the head through Governor vessel and falls as the golden mist (essence with saliva), through the Conception vessel.
The root of life, a source elixir of immortality, where Life turns to Spirit (Ds transformation of Formula [1]) is in the Lower Dan Tian, which is analog to the sea as the origin of life on Earth.

6) The Spirit Root (Shen Gen), where the Primordial Existence turns to manifestation (Dm transformation of Formula [1]) and the Spirit returns to Primordial Existence is in the Upper Dan Tian.

紫清章第二十九
Purple Clarity Chapter   **No. Twenty Nine**

紫 清 上 皇 太 道 君
purple clarity high emperor greatest Tao monarch

太 玄 太 和 侠 侍 端。
greatest mystery greatest union knight serve port

化 生 万 物 使 我 仙
change birth ten thousand things make oneself immortal

飞 升 十 天 驾 玉 轮。
fly ascend ten day harness jade disc

昼 夜 七 日 思 勿 眠
daytime night seven day think do not sleep

子 能 行 此 可 长 存。
child capable walk this can constantly survive

Chapter 2.29

The high emperor of purple clarity and monarch of the Great Tao

is in the greatest mysterious union and vow with his serving knights.[1]

When they change the root of 10,000 things, they make themselves immortal

and fly, ascending, in ten days by harnessing the jade wheel.[2]

They meditate for seven days and nights without sleep,

to give birth to the inner child, capable to walk in Eternity[3].

---

1) We see here a similar principle as in the proverb of Western alchemy: "Justi aquae, Deus mare" (Righteous people are waters, God is the sea). All ancient traditions of knowledge affirm the deep mutual vow between the God and the Virtuous Individuals.

2) The Existence comprised of Uniqueness, Oneness and Individuality (the right axis of the Identity Enhancement symmetry graph on Figure 2), spinning along a designated focus of change.

3) The Immortal Embryo needs to be nurtured until fully developed (the practitioner has to form the own living, void Phase Space of the given body template with all of its 10,000 patterns, or every body cell), before it can merge the Void and walk with Tao. There is a similar message in Bible: "I tell you the truth, no one can enter the kingdom of God unless he is born of water and the Spirit" (the water indicates Jing and Qi, horizontal plane on Figure 4, while spirit, Shen is associated to vertical axis, One's True Nature, Immortal Embryo is formed in the center).

Jī	Gōng	Chéng	Liàn	Fēi	Zì	Rán
积	功	成	炼	非	自	然
store	deeds	accomplish	refine	not be	oneself	natural

Shì	Yóu	Jīng	Chéng	Yì	Yóu	Zhuān
是	由	精	诚	亦	由	专。
be	follow	essence	sincere	also	follow	purpose

Nèi	Shǒu	Jiān	Gù	Zhēn	Zhī	Zhēn
内	守	坚	固	真	之	真
internal	guard	strong	solid	true	's	truth

Xū	Zhōng	Tián	Dàn	Zì	Zhì	Shén
虚	中	恬	淡	自	致	神。
void	middle	peaceful	fresh	oneself	devote	spirit

They naturally amass the good deeds, refining themselves towards perfection,

sincerely regulating the own Great Mission, embedded to their essence.

The Truth within Truth[4] has to be well guarded in order to mature and solidify.

Then in the middle of void, the new, peaceful, fresh spirit starts to live.[5]

---

4) Jing, essence (genetic material at the physical plane) carries the original data, template of Truth to be accomplished. An ideal people can read in the own heart is the accomplishment of the own Mission. A transmutation of Jing (through Qi, Shen and Void to Tao) is the path to connect the pre-defined template with the fully developed system. New self that drives the process of cultivation grows from a central point (see Figure 2) of the transformation circle.

5) A new individual wholeness, at the higher level, a true Presence built upon what we already are and what we aspire to be.

百 谷 章 第 三 十

Bǎi Gǔ Zhāng Dì Sān Shí

Hundred Grain Chapter No. Thirty

百 谷 之 实 土 地 精
Bǎi Gǔ Zhī Shí Tǔ Dì Jīng
hundred grain 's fruit crude Earth essence

五 味 外 美 邪 魔 腥。
Wǔ Wèi Wài Měi Xié Mó Xīng
five flavor external beautiful evil demon fishy

臭 乱 神 明 胎 气 零
Chòu Luàn Shén Míng Tāi Qì Líng
Stink disturb spirit bright fetus Qi wither

那 从 反 老 得 还 婴。
Nà Cóng Fǎn Lǎo Dé Huán Yīng
that from reverse old gain return infant

三 魂 忽 忽 魄 糜 倾
Sān Hún Hū Hū Pò Mí Qīng
three Heaven spirit neglect Earth spirit dissolved collapse

何 不 食 气 太 和 精
Hé Bù Shí Qì Tài Hé Jīng
why not feed Qi Great Harmony essence

故 能 不 死 入 黄 宁。
Gù Néng Bù Sǐ Rù Huáng Níng
Therefore can not die enter yellow peace

228

Chapter 2.30

The substance of the hundred types of grains and fruits comes from Earth essence.

Its five flavors are beautiful outside, but smelly inside.

This smell disturbs the bright fetus spirit and makes its Qi wither.

That which reverses the age helps the spiritual infant to recover.

However, the three Heavenly Spirits (Hun) that ignore the Earth Spirits (Po) eventually also dissove.[1]

So, why not feed from the Qi coming from Greatest Harmony essence[2]

and consequently not die but enter the yellow peace?

---

1) The Three Heavenly sprits are belong the ascension intent and the Liver (see Figure 5), comprising Hun spirit. The Seven Earthly spirits constitute the seven-fold descending spirit of the Lungs (Po). Even though the Heavenly spirits in the body have the more noble direction, they are still connected with Earthly spirits, as a part of the same Five Element cycle.

2) Feeding from the infinite "Power Plant" of Primordial, Great Harmony (Tai He) between Heaven and Earth. The Great Harmony lies in the center of the Five Element cycle, driving both descend into new pairs of conflicts (by Spirits of Earth) and re-integration into higher unity (by Spirits of Heaven).

Xīn Diǎn Yī Tǐ Wǔ Cáng Wáng

心 典 一 体 五 藏 王

heart ceremony one entity five solid organs king

Dòng Jìng Niàn Zhī Dào Dé Xíng

动 静 念 之 道 德 行。

motion silence chant it Tao Virtue prevail

Qīng Jié Xǐ Qì Zì Míng Guāng

清 洁 喜 气 自 明 光

purity clean happiness Qi oneself light radiance

Zuò Qǐ Wú Jù Gòng Dòng Liáng

坐 起 吾 俱 共 栋 梁。

sit rising I altogether share joint pillar

Zhòu Rì Yào Jìng Mù Bì Cáng

昼 日 曜 景 暮 闭 藏

daytime sun glorious scenery dusk close hide

Tōng Lì Huá Jīng Diào Yīn Yáng

通 利 华 精 调 阴 阳。

connect benefit splendid essence harmony Ying Yang

Chapter 2.31

The heart is the king of the five organs and governs the laws of the whole body.[1]

Regardless of whether the function is body motion, silence, or chanting, it's Tao and its Virtue that prevail.

If the heart is honest and clear, the Qi of self-cultivation[2] shines out.

The pivot point of sitting and standing hosts the Individual Spirit.[3]

During the daytime, sun shines on beautiful scenery; at dusk the scene closes and hides.[4]

All the benefits of a radiant essence come from the harmonization of Yin and Yang.[5]

---

1) The heart spirit is Shen, and matches the peak extreme (drives the limits) of the body function (Figure 5). Spleen spirit (Yi) regulates reintegration between the two cycles of body function.

2) The blood from heart nourishes the whole body that is healthy and active. In alchemy, the internally generated Light radiates at the top point of the Five Element transformation cycle (Figure 5).

3) Between the horizontal plane of Life and the vertical axis of the Spirit (Figure 4), True Self finds the seat in the nameless pivot point, the center of the Being (three axis) that connects it to a Non-Being (Dragon on Figure 4).

4) Opening and closing, day and night. are natural aspects of balance/symmetry of all forms of Nature.

5) The essence (Jing) is born from the combination of Yin and Yang, originated from father and mother at physical conception or the Individual Being and Non-Being for the Immortal Embryo.

经 历 章 第 三 十 二
Jīng Lì Zhāng Dì Sān Shí Èr

Scripture Experience Chapter No. Thirty Two

经	历	六	合	隐	卯	酉
Jīng	Lì	Liù	Hé	Yǐn	Mǎo	Yǒu
scripture	history	six	together	secret	Rabbit	Rooster

两	肾	之	神	主	延	寿。
Liǎng	Shèn	Zhī	Shén	Zhǔ	Yán	Shòu
two	kidney	's	spirit	charge	extend	longevity

转	降	适	斗	藏	初	九
Zhuǎn	Jiàng	Shì	Dǒu	Cáng	Chū	Jiǔ
revolve	descend	pursue	Dipper	hide	basic	nine

知	雄	守	雌	可	无	老.
Zhī	Xióng	Shǒu	Cí	Kě	Wú	Lǎo
understand	male	preserve	female	can	no	old

知	白	见	黑	急	坐	守。
Zhī	Bái	Jiàn	Hēi	Jí	Zuò	Shǒu
understand	white	see	black	worry	seat	observe

Chapter 2.32

The Scripture of our Life has six secret harmonies, starting between Mao and You[1] Earthly branch.

The spirit of the two kidneys is in charge of extending longevity,

it manages the collection of the first Nine, by revolving and congealing essence[2], according to Big Dipper movements.

Understand the male aspect and preserve the female aspect and you will know no aging.[3]

Understand white, research black, carefully guarding your meditation seat.[4]

---

1) Fourth (Mao, Rabbit) and tenth (You, Rooster) Earthy branches (see Glossary), that geometrically lie in 180 degrees (east and west), marking the start of the day (and the spin of elementary circle). There are other five pairs of Earthly branches.

2) The action of exchanging polarities in individual "spin" (IE symmetry) reflects in congealing the form. Two kidneys are like a natural electromagnetic battery, each representing one pole. The spinning of Post-Heaven Qi between them generates new Pre-Heaven Qi (to flow through Microcosmic orbit) in between (at Ming Men), similar to the way electronic current is generated between two rotating magnets.

3) Action/function (male aspect) - the structure of the magnetic field needs to be well set up, while substance/carrying medium (charge, female aspect) has to be preserved, so that electric current should not leak. Once this is done, mutually orthogonal male and female aspects will support each other and can extend existence of Individuality, similar to an orthogonally polarized magnetic and electric field passing through space.

4) The place of the True Man, between Yin and Yang aspects: the current manifestation symmetries on the one side and eternal cultivation on the other (horizontal and vertical axis on Figure 2).

肝气章第三十三
Gān Qì Zhāng Dì Sān Shí Sān
Liver Qi Chapter No. Thirty Three

肝 气 郁 勃 清 且 长
Gān Qì Yù Bó Qīng Qiě Cháng
Liver Qi luxuriant vigorous clear and eternal

罗 列 六 府 生 三 光。
Luó Liè Liù Fǔ Shēng Sān Guāng
gather list six mansion birth three light

心 精 意 专 内 不 倾
Xīn Jīng Yì Zhuān Nèi Bù Qīng
Heart essence intent focus internal not collapse

上 合 三 焦 下 玉 浆。
Shàng Hé Sān Jiāo Xià Yù Jiāng
above join Triple Heater below Jade Paste

玄 液 云 行 去 臭 香
Xuán Yè Yún Xíng Qù Chòu Xiāng
mysterious liquid cloudy walk rid stinky smell

治 荡 发 齿 炼 五 方。
Zhì Dàng Fā Chǐ Liàn Wǔ Fāng
control dissolute hair tooth practice five direction

取 津 玄 膺 入 明 堂
Qǔ Jīn Xuán Yīng Rù Míng Táng
take saliva Mysterious Source enter Light Hall

Chapter 2.33

Liver Qi is fine, vigorous, bright and everlasting.

Gather an arrangement of six mansions, give birth to the three lights.[1]

The Nature of the heart essence is directed internally to avoid collapse.[2]

Above it joins the Triple Burner, below it joins the source of the Jade Paste.

Mysterious cloudy liquid constantly circulates and eliminates the stagnant Qi.

Prevent a dissolution of the teeth and hair by practicing biting in five directions.

Bring the saliva from the Mystical Well to front and upwards, into the Hall of Light.[3]

---

1) Between the Yin and Yang aspect of each of three treasures (Jing, Qi, Shen), the practitioner can in meditation find and transform them in Three Dan Tian.

2) Contractions of the physical heart send blood through body. Gathering of the Spirit causes stirring and flow of Qi.

3) Saliva (carrier of essence/Jing) emerges underneath mouth (Xuan Ying – Mystical Well), which is associated with the spleen (and Earth element) and flows up the tongue to the upper Dan Tian (Ming Tang – Hall of Light). The upward flowing fluid of Earth is there integrated with the descending energy of Heaven (Kong Qi from air) to strengthen the body.

| Xià 下 below | Gài 溉 irrigate | Hóu 喉 pharynx | Lóng 咙 throat | Shén 神 intelligent | Míng 明 understandable | Tōng 通 |

| Zuò 坐 sit | Shì 侍 attend | Huá 华 splendid | Gài 盖 canopy | Yóu 游 tour | Guì 贵 noble | Jīng 京 capital |

| Piāo 飘 float | Piāo 飘 drift | Sān 三 three | Dì 帝 emperor | Xí 席 feast | Qīng 清 clear | Liáng 凉 cool |

| Wǔ 五 five | Sè 色 color | Yún 云 cloud | Qì 气 Qi | Fēn 纷 profuse | Qīng 青 green | Cōng 葱 scallion |

| Bì 闭 close | Mù 目 eye | Nèi 内 internal | Miàn 眄 look | Zì 自 self | Xiāng 相 mutual | Wàng 望。observe |

| Shǐ 使 make | Xīn 心 heart | Zhū 诸 all | Shén 神 spirit | Huán 还 still | Xiāng 相 mutually | Chóng 崇 respect |

| Qī 七 seven | Xuán 玄 mystery | Yīng 英 brave | Huá 华 flower | Kāi 开 open | Mìng 命 life | Mén 门。gate |

| Tōng 通 know | Lì 利 benefit | Tiān 天 Heavenly | Dào 道 Tao | Cún 存 keep | Xuán 玄 mysterious | Gēn 根 root |

Then let it drop down the throat to establish the bright spiritual pathway.

It will then nourish the Splendid Canopy[4] and roam to the precious Capital City,[5]

and flow around the seats of the three emperors, making them clear and cool.[6]

A Qi cloud of five colors will nourish the green growth.[7]

With closed eyes, meditate on the vision of yourself at the full moon,

making it possible for all spirits to integrate in the heart,[8] with mutual devotion.

When seven mysterious flowers blossom, the life gate will open.[9]

Understand the benefits of Heavenly Tao and nurture the mysterious root.[10]

---

4) Lungs (Metal Element), diaphragm and Medium Dan Tian

5) Lower Dan Tian

6) Three channels around Dan Tian, connected it to Kidneys (Water Element) and genitals.

7) Giving new life to the Liver (Wood Element).

8) The vitality from saliva then invigorates the Heart (the highest extreme of body function, belonging to the Fire Element), completing an overall four season integration.

9) When the seven important centers mentioned (mouth, Upper, Middle and Lower Dan Tian, liver, kidney, and heart) are invigorated, the Ming Men (life gate) will open for a flow of elixir.

百 二 十 年 犹 可 还。
Bǎi Èr Shí Nián Yóu Kě Huán
hundred twenty year still can return

过 此 守 道 诚 独 难
Guò Cǐ Shǒu Dào Chéng Dú Nán
cross this keep Tao sincerely alone difficult

唯 待 九 转 八 琼 丹。
Wéi Dài Jiǔ Zhuǎn Bā Qióng Dān
only wait nine revolve eight jade pellet

要 复 精 思 存 七 元
Yào Fù Jīng Sī Cún Qī Yuán
want recover essence thought keep seven origins

日 月 之 华 救 老 残。
Rì Yuè Zhī Huá Jiù Lǎo Cán
Sun Moon 's splendor save old injury

肝 气 周 流 络 无 端。
Gān Qì Zhōu Liú Luò Wú Duān
liver Qi circular flow net no end

Even hundred and twenty year old people can thus still rejuvenate.

If you do not follow this practice, preserving the Tao is truly difficult.

You only need nine revolutions for the each of eight jade pills.[10]

For recovery of essence, mentally deposit elixir to the seven origins.

The splendor of the Sun and Moon can heal old injuries.

The flow of Liver Qi through the network of internal channels never ends.

---

10) Totally swallow 72 times for this practice (see Figure 9)

肺 之 章 第 三 十 四
Fèi Zhī Zhāng Dì Sān Shí Sì

Lung 's Chapter No. Thirty Four

肺 之 为 气 三 焦 起。
Fèi Zhī Wéi Qì Sān Jiāo Qǐ

Lung 's act Qi Triple Heater start

视 听 幽 冥 候 童 子。
Shì Tīng Yōu Míng Hòu Tóng Zǐ

watch listen serene deep await boy

调 理 五 华 精 发 齿
Diào Lǐ Wǔ Huá Jīng Fā Chǐ

recuperate order five splendor essence hair tooth

三 十 六 咽 玉 池 里。
Sān Shí Liù Yān Yù Chí Lǐ

thirty six swallow jade pool within

开 通 百 脉 血 液 始
Kāi Tōng Bǎi Mài Xuè Yè Shǐ

open up hundred vessel blood liquid start

颜 色 生 光 金 玉 泽。
Yán Sè Shēng Guāng Jīn Yù Zé

face appear shininess light gold jade luster

Chapter 2.34

Qi originates in the Triple Burner (San Jiao) and is
directed by the Lungs.[1]

Wait, patiently meditating on the center between the
Kidneys, and the Qi would emerge as a feeling of the young
child,

and rejuvenate body tissues, invigorate the essence of the
five organs, the hair, and the teeth.

Swallow the jade pool liquid 36 times into the internal
void.[2]

Thus open up 100 blood vessels so the flow will be smooth.

The face will radiate light, resembling the shine of gold and
jade.

---

1) This chapter describes the overall flow of Qi, in a similar way as
the previous chapter described the circulation of Jing.

2) The Lower Dan Tian.

Chǐ	Jiān	Fā	Hēi	Bù	Zhī	Bái
齿	坚	发	黑	不	知	白
tooth	strong	hair	dark	not	know	white
Cún	Cǐ	Zhēn	Shén	Wù	Luò	Luò
存	此	真	神	勿	落	落。
keep	this	true	spirit	not	allow	fall
Dāng	Yì	Cǐ	Gōng	Yǒu	Zuò	Xí
当	忆	此	宫	有	座	席
shall	remember	this	palace	there is		seat
Zhòng	Shén	Hé	Huì	Zhuǎn	Xiāng	Suǒ
众	神	合	会	转	相	索。
all	spirit	jointly	meet	turn	mutually	seek

242

The teeth will recover their strength and the hair will become dark without any gray.

Store this true spirit within, not letting it go out.

It should be deposited to its seat in the palace.[3]

All other body spirits will resolve around it, demanding each other.[4]

---

3) The cross point between symmetry and asymmetry of the body, the lower Dan Tian.

4) Center of the flow of five the element generation/restriction cycle and other identity enhancement symmetries within the body.

隐藏章第三十五

Yǐn Cáng Zhāng Dì Sān Shí Wǔ

Conceal Hide Chapter — No. Thirty Five

隐	藏	羽	盖	看	天	舍
Yǐn	Cáng	Yǔ	Gài	Kàn	Tiān	Shè
conceal	hide	feather	cover	watch	Heavenly	home

朝	拜	太	阳	乐	相	呼。
Zhāo	Bài	Tài	Yáng	Lè	Xiāng	Hū
morning	worship	great	Yang	happily	mutually	breathe

明	神	八	威	正	辟	邪
Míng	Shén	Bā	Wēi	Zhèng	Bì	Xié
wise	spirit	eight	power	upright	dispel	evil

脾	神	还	归	是	胃	家。
Pí	Shén	Huán	Guī	Shì	Wèi	Jiā
spleen	spirit	return		is	stomach	home

耽	养	灵	根	不	复	枯
Dān	Yǎng	Líng	Gēn	Bù	Fù	Kū
delay	nurture	spiritual	root	not	return	wither

闭	塞	命	门	保	玉	都。
Bì	Sāi	Mìng	Mén	Bǎo	Yù	Dū
close	lock	life	gate	preserve	jade	capital

万	神	方	胙	寿	有	余
Wàn	Shén	Fāng	Zuò	Shòu	Yǒu	Yú
10000	spirit	upright	bestow	longevity	have	surplus

Chapter 2.35

Hide within the created feather cover to look after the Heavenly home.[1]

In the morning, worship happily, inhale and exhale the Great Yang.

The eight powers of the shining spirit of wisdom will dispel evil.

The return point of the spleen spirit is the home of the stomach.[2]

If you neglect this nurturing process,[3] the spiritual root will not be restored and it will wither.

Close and lock the gate of life to preserve the jade capital.

Longevity and prosperity are bestowed through a surplus of 10,000 spirits[4].

---

1) The feather cover (energy around the body) completes the development of the personal field and merges with the Universe.

2) Content/substance (spleen) and form/function (stomach) are female (Yin) and male (Yang) aspects of the Earth element in the body, integrated into family (wife and husband) harmony. The Yin also symbolizes division and new forms in the Universe, the Yang symbolizes re-integration and return to Tao.

3) This chapter describes the revolution of Spirit (Shen) (complementing the circulation of Qi in Chapter 34 and essence/Jing in Chapter 33).

4) The substance borrowed from the Universe during growth of an Individual needs to be returned, but the internally generated Jing-Qi-Shen replica of the body cells bestows the longevity.

Shì 是 is	Wèi 谓 say	Pí 脾 spleen	Jiàn 建 build	Zài 在 in	Zhōng 中 middle	Gōng 宫。 palace
Wǔ 五 five	Cáng 藏 organs	Liù 六 six	Fǔ 府 organs	Shén 神 spirit	Míng 明 intelligent	Zhǔ 主 charge
Shàng 上 above	Hé 合 join	Tiān 天 Heaven	Mén 门 gate	Rù 入 enter	Míng 明 Light	Táng 堂。 Hall
Shǒu 守 keep	Cí 雌 female	Cún 存 preserve	Xióng 雄 male	Dǐng 顶 carry	Sān 三 three	Guāng 光 light
Wài 外 external	Fāng 方 square	Nèi 内 internal	Yuán 圆 round	Shén 神 spirit	Zài 在 in	Zhōng 中。 middle
Tōng 通 understand	Lì 利 benefit	Xuè 血 blood	Mài 脉 pulse	Wǔ 五 five	Cáng 藏 solid organs	Fēng 丰 rich
Gǔ 骨 bone	Qīng 青 green	Jīn 筋 tendon	Chì 赤 red	Suǐ 髓 marrow	Rú 如 seem	Shuāng 霜。 frost
Pí 脾 spleen	Jiù 救 assist	Qī 七 seven	Qiào 窍 aperture	Qù 去 get rid	Bù 不 not	Xiáng 祥 auspicious

The spleen is designated to build up the void in a middle palace.[5]

Five solid and six hollow organs are hosted by a spirit of intelligence.

Joined to the Heavens above through the gateway point at upper palate.[6]

Adjoin female and store male essence to support the three lights.

The spirit is in the middle of the external square and an internal circle.

Connect to goodness through the blood pulse, and make five solid organs abundant.

The bones will rejuvenate, tendons will empower and marrow will be washed from impurities.

The spleen will ensure that all that is not auspicious is expelled through the seven apertures.

---

5) The fifth element, Earth (organ spleen), governs the completion of each four-fold cycle, collecting impressions from the passage and generating Pre-Heaven from Post-Heaven Qi (as in the Bhagavad Gita: "Eat the reminder of the sacrifice and you would be free from any sin"). True sacrifice is, of course, always one of internal alchemy, as we don't really own anything external.

6) Ming Tang, Hall of Brightness.

日月列布设阴阳。

两神相会化玉英

淡然无味天人粮。

子丹进馔肴正黄

乃曰琅膏及玉霜。

太上隐环八素琼

溉益八液肾受精。

伏于太阴见我形

The Sun and Moon arrangements provide a template how to set up internal Yin and Yang.

The two spirits will meet each other and change into Jade Liquid.[7]

The food of Heavenly man is neutral and has no flavor.

The inner elixir receives its delicacy straight from the center,[8]

which can be called gem soup, or jade frost,[9]

most of all, from the secret ring of eight-fold plain jade.

Ingest the benefits of eight liquids, and the Kidneys will conceive essence.

Lean over the Greatest Yin, see one's own image.

---

7) The ethereal aspect of saliva.

8) Huang Ya: elixir food, the Totality Centering principle.

9) The transcendental nourishment that is a void complement of the manifested patterns.

扬 Yáng	风 Fēng	三 Sān	玄 Xuán	出 Chū	始 Shǐ	青。 Qīng
spread	wind	three	mystery	out	start	green

恍 Huǎng	惚 Hū	之 Zhī	间 Jiān	至 Zhì	清 Qīng	灵 Líng
Absent-minded	's	between	reach	clear	spirit

戏 Xì	于 Yú	飙 Biāo	台 Tái	见 Jiàn	赤 Chì	生。 Shēng
show	at	whirlwind	stage	see	red	birth

逸 Yì	城 Chéng	熙 Xī	真 Zhēn	养 Yǎng	华 Huá	荣 Róng
leisure	city	prosperous	true	nurture	splendid	honor

内 Nèi	盼 Pàn	沉 Chén	默 Mò	炼 Liàn	五 Wǔ	形。 Xíng
internal	expect	immerse	silent	refine	five	image

三 Sān	气 Qì	徘 Pái	徊 Huái	得 Dé	神 Shén	明 Míng
three	Qi	hover	irresolute	gain	spirit	intelligent

隐 Yǐn	龙 Lóng	遁 Dùn	芝 Zhī	云 Yún	琅 Láng	英。 Yīng
hide	dragon	flee	Ganoderma	cloud	jade	bravery

可 Kě	以 Yǐ	充 Chōng	饥 Jī	使 Shǐ	万 Wàn	灵 Líng
able	fill	satisfy	hunger	make	10,000	spirit,

Spread the wind of three mysteries out of emerging youth,

unattached and without thoughts between the breezes of the clear spirit.

Take a seat at the whirlwind stage and observe the primordial birth.

In the leisure region, true prosperity supports a splendid honor.[10]

Internal dedication to a deep silence is refined by five images.

Three Qi hover irresolutely to attract the intelligent spirit.

The dragon is hiding, disappearing in a Medicine[11] Cloud to achieve the Jade Courage.

In order to satisfy hunger, employ 10,000 spirits.

---

10) Transcendental transformation: prosperity bringing peace is transmuted to new prosperity born from peace.

11) The original says "Ganoderma mushroom," which is an ancient Chinese symbol of health. Dragon is a symbol of the Individual Void that develops, in every development cycle through a new set of of Mysteries (driven by the various spiritual principles).

Shàng	Gài	Xuán	Xuán	Xià	Hǔ	Zhāng
上	盖	玄	玄	下	虎	章。
above	cover	mystery	mystery	below	tiger	seal

Above, there will be mystery within mystery, below the tiger seal.[12]

---

12) Symbol of authority that used to be given to commanding officers (in this case incarnated spirit) from their sovereign (in this case a Primordial Spirit of the Individual).

沐浴章 第三十六
Mù Yù Zhāng Dì Sān Shí Liù

Cleansing Bath   Chapter   No. Thirty Six

沐	浴	盛	洁	弃	肥	薰
Mù	Yù	Shèng	Jié	Qì	Féi	Xūn
cleansing	bath	contain	clean	abandon	fertile	fragrance

入	室	东	向	诵	玉	篇。
Rù	Shì	Dōng	Xiàng	Sòng	Yù	Piān
enter	room	east	toward	recite	jade	chapter

约	得	万	遍	义	自	鲜
Yuē	Dé	Wàn	Biàn	Yì	Zì	Xiān
about	gain	10000	time	meaning	self	fresh

散	发	无	欲	以	长	存。
Sàn	Fā	Wú	Yù	Yǐ	Cháng	Cún
loose	hair	no	lust	so that	long	live

五	味	皆	至	正	气	还
Wǔ	Wèi	Jiē	Zhì	Zhèng	Qì	Huán
five	flavor	all	take	healthy	Qi	return

夷	心	寂	闷	勿	烦	冤。
Yí	Xīn	Jì	Mèn	Wù	Fán	Yuān
foreign	heart	lonely	stuffy	do not	trouble	wrong

Chapter 2.36

A cleansing bath contains a clearing abundance of fertile fragrance.

Enter the room facing east and reciting the Jade Writing.

Go through it 10,000 times, trying to understand its meaning, to refresh yourself.

Loosen your hair, have no lust, so you can live forever.

Circulate all five flavors until healthy Qi returns.[1]

Cleanse the heart through distant purity; have no worries or concerns.

---

1) Primordial, neutral Qi, gathered between the Five Elements

Guò	Shù	Yǐ	Bì	Tǐ	Shén	Jīng
过	数	已	毕	体	神	精
pass	number	already	complete	body	spirit	essence

Huáng	Huá	Yù	Nǚ	Gào	Zǐ	Qíng
黄	华	玉	女	告	子	情。
yellow	splendor	jade	girl	tell	child	passion

Zhēn	Rén	Jì	Zhì	Shǐ	Liù	Dīng
真	人	既	至	使	六	丁
true	man	since	arrive	send	six	man

Jí	Shòu	Yǐn	Zhī	Dà	Dòng	Jīng
即	受	隐	芝	大	洞	经。
Promptly	receive	latent	ganoderma	big	cave	scripture

Shí	Dú	Sì	Bài	Zhāo	Tài	Shàng
十	读	四	拜	朝	太	上。
ten	read	four	worship	toward	ancient	above

Xiān	Yè	Tài	Dì	Hòu	Běi	Xiàng
先	谒	太	帝	后	北	向
first	call	on	ancient	emperor	then north	direction

Huáng	Tíng	Nèi	Jīng	Yù	Shū	Chàng
黄	庭	内	经	玉	书	畅。
yellow	court	internal	scripture	jade	book	smooth

Shòu	Zhě	Yuē	Shī	Shòu	Zhě	Méng
授	者	曰	师	受	者	盟
teach	individual	call	teacher	receive	individual	pledge

256

Circulate full Qi through the body between spirit and essence.

The brilliant Jade Girl in the center will talk to you with newborn passion.

True Man[2] would arrive and instruct the six aspects.

Readily accept secret medicine, the writing from the great cave.

Ten times read, four times worship the ancient from above.

Evoke the greatest ancient emperor and face North.

If unimpeded by inner obstacles, Yellow Court Internal Scripture will become the Jade Writing.[3]

Do not personally instruct others in it until you receive their oath of sincerity.

---

2) One's own higher self.

3) Jade writing is the Internal Receiving of the External Words of Wisdom (that can be different for any individual). Writing indicates bodily understanding by a practitioner that is, through an internal alchemy (balancing the manifestation of the noble spiritual principles on Earth), written to his/her chapter of the Book of Truth (the established set of symmetries in Heaven).

Yún	Jǐn	Fèng	Luó	Jīn	Niǔ	Chán
云	锦	凤	罗	金	钮	缠。
cloud	brocade	phoenix	silk	golden	button	twine

Yǐ	Dài	Gē	Fā	Jī	Fū	Quán
以	代	割	发	肌	肤	全
with	replace	cut	hair	muscle	skin	whole

Xié	Shǒu	Dēng	Shān	Shà	Yè	Dān
携	手	登	山	歃	液	丹。
take	hand	climb	mountain	drink	liquid	elixir

Jīn	Shū	Yù	Jǐng	Nǎi	Kě	Xuān
金	书	玉	景	乃	可	宣
golden	book	jade	scenery	then	can	proclaim

Chuán	Dé	Kě	Shòu	Gào	Sān	Guān
传	得	可	授	告	三	官。
convey	permit	can	give	report	three	official

Wù	Líng	Qī	Zǔ	Shòu	Míng	Huàn
勿	令	七	祖	受	冥	患
do not	make	seven	ancestor	suffer	obscure	sickness

Tài	Shàng	Wēi	Yán	Zhì	Shén	Xiān
太	上	微	言	致	神	仙
ancient	above	subtle	speech	reach	spirit	immortal

Bù	Sǐ	Zhī	Dào	Cǐ	Zhēn	Jīng
不	死	之	道	此	真	经。
no death		is	Tao	this	true	scripture

A token needs to be wrapped in the cloud brocade and phoenix silk, fastened with golden button.

A lock of cut hair will replace the commitment of the flesh and blood.

Take the student's hand and climb the mountain together, to drink the elixir.

Then you can explain the jade scenery of the book of gold.

Pass it on to suitable people who can offer their achievement to the three purities[4]

but not to those who would burden the seven ancestors.[5]

This scripture passes speech from above, intended for Individual immortal spirits to listen.

"No Death" is the Tao of this True Writing.[6]

---

4) Who are capable of Oneness-Uniqueness-Individuality transformation, as a noble continuation of previous high work.

5) Do not pass the knowledge to those who you think would use it for lower, selfish purposes and desires, just making problems for others and themselves.

6) Negation of the negative gives a positive, a void within void generates an existence. This is a way of Nature.
    An inherent, ultimate mission of any mortal being is to challenge and conquer death (in the way of a true warrior who continually fights his own shadow, the overall inner absurd or cultivation corruption factor), not the other beings.
    Most spiritual traditions agree about it and St. Paul, says in Bible: "The last enemy to be destroyed is death".
    This era of the great advancements of knowledge is probably a good time for the mankind to pick up that fight and win.

APPENDIX

Original Calligraphy Plates by Wang Xizhi

Wang Xizhi (王羲之) is considered a Sage of Calligraphy (书圣) in China. He lived in the 4th century C.E. and had been also a general and an imperial officer in the Jin Dynasty. He studied many calligraphy styles of previous dynasties and tried to reproduce and extend them in his personal style, which was described by experts as very fluid and full of quiet beauty. Reproduction of the old Huang Ting Jing scripture is one of his famous works

上有黃庭下有關元前有幽關後有命門

噓吸廬外出入丹田審能行之可長存黃庭

中人衣朱衣關門壯籥蓋兩扉幽關俠之

高巍巍丹田之中精氣微玉池清水上上肥靈

黄庭経

上有黄庭下關元後有幽闕前有命盧呼吸盧間外出

入丹田審能行之可長存黄庭中人衣朱衣關門壯籥

盖兩扉幽闕俠之高巍巍丹田之中精氣微玉池清水上

生肥靈根堅志不衰中池有士服赤朱橫下三寸神所居

中外相距重閉之神廬之中務脩治玄膺氣管受精符

急固子精以自持宅中有士常衣絳子能見之可不病橫

理長尺約其上子能守之可無恙呼噏廬間以自償保守

冤堅身受慶方寸之中謹蓋藏精神還歸老復壯俠

幽關流下竟養子玉樹不可杖至道不煩不旁迕

靈臺通天臨中野方寸之中至關下玉房之中神門戶

既是公子教我者明堂四達法海源真人子丹當我前

三關之間精氣深子欲不死脩崑崙絳宮重樓十二級

宮室之中五采集赤神之子中池立下有長城玄谷邑長

生要則房中急棄捐逍遙欲專守精寸田尺宅可治生繫

子長流志安寧觀志流神三奇靈閒暇無事心太平

常存玉房視明達時念大倉不飢渴役使六丁神女

謂閉子精路可長活正室之中神所居洗心自治無敢

汙廬觀五藏視節度六府脩治潔如素虛無自然□

之故物有自然事不煩垂共無為心自安體虛無之居

在廬間寂莫曠然口不言恬惔無為遊德園積精香

潔玉女存作道憂柔以獨居扶養性命守虛無恬惔

無為何思慮羽翼以成正扶疏長生久視乃飛去五行

參差同根節三五合氣要本一誰與共之升日月抱珠

候以和子室子自有之持無失即得不亡藏金室出月

入日是吾道天七地三回相守升降五行一合九玉石落是

吾寶子自有之何不守心曉根帶養華采服天順地

合藏精七日之奇五連相合崐崘之性不迷誤九源之

山何亭之中人有真人可使令薇之蕊宮丹城樓俠以日月

如明珠萬歲眙以非有期外本三陽神自来內養三神

可長生魂欲上天魄入淵還魂反魄道自然提瓈懸珠

環無端玉石戶金籥身完堅戴地玄天迣乾坤象以四

時未如丹前御後卑各異門送以還丹與玄泉象龜別

却致六獄中仔真人巾金巾負甲持符開七門此非枝

葉寶是根晝夜思之可長存仙人道士非可神積精所

人為身作人皆食穀與五味獨食太和陰陽氣故能不

死天相既心為國主五藏王受意動靜氣行行道自守

我精神光晝日照夜自守渴自得飲飢自飽經應此

周藏外胃轉陽之陰藏於九常能行之不知老竓之

為氣調且長羅列五藏生三光上合三焦道飲醴泉我

神魂魄在中央隨鼻上下知肥香立於懸雍通明堂

伏於玄門候天道近在於身還自守精神上下關分

理通利天地長生道古孔已通不知老還空陰陽天門

候陰陽下于嚨喉通神明過華蓋下清且涼入清泠

267

淵見吾形期成還丹可長生還過華池動腎精立于明
堂臨丹田將使諸神開命門通利天道至靈根陰陽
列布如流星肺之為氣三焦起上眼伏天門候故道自
視天地存童子調和精華理髮齒顏色潤澤不復白
下于嚨喉何落諸神皆會相求索下有絳宮紫華
色隱在華蓋通神盧專守心神轉相好觀我諸神辟
除邪偲神還歸依大家至於胃管通虛無閉塞命門
如玉都壽專萬歲浮有餘脾中之神舍中宮上伏令
閉合明堂通利六府調五行金木水火土為王日月列宿

張陰陽二神相得下玉英五藏為王腎最尊伏於大陰

成其形出入二竅舍黄庭呼吸虛無見吾形强我筋骨

血脈盛恖恍不見過清靈恬快無欲遂得生還於七

門飲太淵亰我玄雍過清靈閒我仙道與奇方頭戴

母素跙丹田沐浴華池生靈根被髮行之可長存三府

相得開命門五味皆至開善氣還常能行之可長生

永和十二年五月廿四日五山陰縣寫

269

GLOSSARY

The list below provides a brief definition of some very common terms of Chinese Alchemy that are, due to their complexity of meaning, often referenced literally throughout current translation and comments, without attempting to define matching English terms.

八卦 **Ba Gua** – "eight trigrams" of "Yi Jing", time components of change, or Feng Shui corners, each has associated unique number in octal (numbers 0-7) and binary base system (000-111) that can be also represented as binary number matching the trigram lines (with the full, yang line represented by 1 and the broken, yin line by 0), looking from bottom (inside) to top (outside).

乾 ☰ – Heaven, creativity, octal number 7 (binary 111)

兑 ☱ – Lake, cloud, wealth, 6 (110)

离 ☲ – Fire, beauty, lightning, 5 (101)

震 ☳ – Thunder, transformation, 4 (100)

巽 ☴ – Wind, distribution, 3 (011)

坎 ☵ – Water, container, abyss, 2 (010)

艮 ☶ – Mountain, formation, structure, 1 (001)

坤 ☷ – Earth, substance, receptivity, 0 (000)

丹田 **Dan Tian** – "field of elixir", the area within body where spirit and energy are merged for cultivation purposes. There are three Dan Tians (upper, medium, and lower, residing loosely in the forehead, heart and abdomen, matching the three Yoga Maha Marmas). Without an attribute (higher, medium, lower), the term assumes lower Dan Tian, the geometrical and gravity center of the body, where the cultivation transcendence has a physical source.

地支 ^{Dì Zhī} **Earthly Branches** – 12 phases of day or year, corresponding to Chinese Zodiac animals and acupuncture meridians:

丑 ^{Chǒu} - 1-3 a.m. Chou (Bull) Liver

寅 ^{Yín} - 3-5 a.m. Yin (Tiger) Lung

卯 ^{Mǎo} - 5-7 a.m. Mao (Rabitt) Large Intestine

辰 ^{Chén} - 7-9 a.m. Chen (Dragon) Stomach

巳 ^{Sì} - 9-11 a.m. Si (Snake) Spleen

午 ^{Wǔ} - 11-1 p.m. Wu (Horse) Heart

未 ^{Wèi} - 1-3 p.m. Wei (Sheep) Small Intestine

申 ^{Shēn} - 3-5 p.m.   Shen (Monkey) Urinary Bladder

酉 ^{Yǒu} - 5-7 p.m.   You (Ruster) Kidney

戌 ^{Xū} - 7-9 p.m.   Xu (Dog) Pericardium

亥 ^{Hài} - 9-11 p.m. Hai (Boar) Triple Warmer

子 ^{Zǐ} - 11-1 a.m. Zi (Rat) Gall bladder

五行 ^{Wǔ Xíng} **Five Elements or Phases** – agents of a specific type of action (wood, fire, earth, metal, and water, type of change or angles of derivation, described in the Introduction), sides of the world (east, south, west, north, and center), that correspond to the five organs that produce and store Qi and the five spirits.

木 Mù – Wood, East, Rising, spirit 魂 Hún in liver 肝 Gān

火 Huǒ – Fire, South, High Extreme, spirit 神 Shén in heart 心 Xīn

土 Tǔ – Earth, Center, Pivot, spirit 意 Yì in spleen 脾 Pí

金 Jīn – Metal, West, Descending, spirit 魄 Pò in lungs 肺 Fèi

水 Shuǐ – Water, North, Low Extreme, spirit 志 Zhì in kidneys 肾 Shèn

天干 Tiān Gān **Heavenly Stems –** 10 Yin and Yang aspects of the Five elements, reintegrated through alchemy.

甲 Jiǎ – yang wood

乙 Yǐ – yin wood

丙 Bǐng – yang fire

丁 Dīng – yin fire

戊 Wù – yang earth

己 Jǐ – yin earth

庚 Gēng – yang metal

辛 Xīn – yin metal

壬 Rén – yang water

癸 Guǐ – yin water

Xiān Tiān Hòu Tiān
先天，后天 Pre-Heaven and Post-Heaven represent

realms of established harmony (symmetry) outside of physical manifestation (accrued virtue, before birth) and the manifested, "processing" (everyday world, after birth) world of cultivation of the new level of harmony and virtue, respectively. "True Man" sits in the Pre-Heaven realm, while cultivating Post-Heaven aspects.

Jing Qì Shén
精气神 Three Treasures (Jing, Qi, Shen) – basic elements

of human existence in Taoist and TCM view that can be cultivated and brought to higher levels. Jing stands for essence, the constitutional factor of the body, Qi stands for life force, the vital energy in living organisms or the energy of alignment of the inorganic world, that keeps the body (flow of Jing) together, while Shen represents intellectual and spiritual qualities of the individual.

Tài Jí
太极 Tai Chi – Supreme Absolute, principle, and martial art

where natural balance (achieved symmetry in the Highest Purity realm) of polarities is developed to the maximum, the highest alignment of the Individual to the Tao.

Dào
道 Tao – highest concept and aspired quality that cannot be

described, even though its effects can (indicating different types of Divine interaction with Nature). According to Lu Dong Bin (author of "The Secret of Golden Flower"): "That which exists through itsel.f" Long before developing the religious elements in China, Taoism was considered just as a "Way of Living," i.e., a set of the best (immortal) living practices.

Yīn Yáng
阴阳 Yin Yang – two dualities, complementary opposites that

support and reflect each other, two sides of any symmetry, literally: the shadow and sunny side of the hill. The two main TCM "Extraordinary" vessels are also divided to the Yang Governing

Vessel (or GV, which goes from the perineum, Hui Yin point, up the back, between shoulder blades to the top of the head and down the face into the upper palate) and Yin, or Conception, Vessel (that descends from the upper palate down the front of the body, around the genitals to the perineum).

^{Zhēn} ^{Rén}
真人 **Zhen Ren** – "True Man" (sometimes translated as Sage or "Elevated Man"), one who is continually aware of his higher nature and acts accordingly. Relies on Truth, researches Mystery, and works with the Tao to continuously work on the cultivation of both individual and general Virtue.

BIBLIOGRAPHY

1. Asclepius or the Perfect Sermon (by Hermes Trismegistos, published by Kessinger Publishing, LLC 2005, ISBN 978-1425350208)

2. Bhagavad Gita (translated by Sir Edwin Arnold, publisher: Echo Library 2008, ISBN 978-1848301597)

3. Consciousness or Truth (by Charles Berner and Mona Sosna, http://www.charlesberner.org/Design/manual.html)

4. Fragments (by Heraclitus, translated by Brooks Haxton, foreword by James Hillman, publisher Penguin Group USA 2003, ISBN 9780142437650)

5. Holding Yin, Embracing Yang (translated by Eva Wong, published by Shambhala 2005, ISBN 1-59030-263-X)

6. Holy Bible, King James Version Old & New Testaments (publisher: Visions Design 2009, ASIN: B002920ZOS)

7. Jade Emperor's Mind Seal Classic, (by Stuart Alve Olson, published by Inner Traditions 2003, ISBN 089281135-8)

8. Magick, Book IV (by Aleister Crowley et al, published by Red Wheel/Weiser LLC, 1994, ISBN 0-87728-919-0)

9. My Inventions: The Autobiography of Nikola Tesla (by Nikola Tesla, published by Wilder Publications 2007, ISBN 9781934451779)

10. Mysterium Coniunctionis (by C.G. Jung, published by Princeton/Bollingen Paperbacks 1970, ISBN 0-691-01816-2)

11. Plotinus: The Enneads (by Plotinus and Lorenz Books, published by Larson Publications, 2004, ISBN 978-0943914558)

12. Psychology and Alchemy (by C.G. Jung, published by Princeton/Bollingen Paperbacks 1968, ISBN 0-691-01831-6)

13. Rootless Tree (by Zhang San Feng, translated by Akrishi, http://webspace.webring.com/people/da/akrishi/sanfeng/rt_intro.htm)

14. The Book of Sacred Magic of the Abramelin the Mage (translated by S.L. MacGregor Mathers 1897, reprint by Dover Publications 1975, ISBN: 0-85030-255-2)

15. The Lord of the Rings (by J.R.R. Tolkien, published by Houghton Mifflin 2005, ISBN: 978-0618574995)

16. Spiritual Pivot (by Ling Shu, published by Wu Jing-Nuan 1993, ISBN 978-0-8248-2631-4)

17. Schrödinger's Universe (by Milo Wolff, published by Outskirts Press 2008, ISBN 978-1-4327-1979-1)

18. Tao of Physics (by Fritjof Capra, published by Shambhala 2000, ISBN 1-57062-519-0)

19. Tao Te Ching (by Lao Zi, translated by Gia-Fu Feng, Jane English, published by Vintage 1989, ISBN 978-0679724346)

20. Taoist Texts: Ethical, Political and Specultative (by Balfour, Frederick, published by Tribner and Co./Kelly and Walsh, 1894, ISBN: 9781606201558)

21. The Fire from Within (by Carlos Castaneda, published by Black Swan 1984, ISBN 0-552-99160-0)

22. The Golden Dawn (by Israel Regardie, published by Llewellyn Publications 1986, ISBN 0-87542-663-8)

23. The Key of Solomon the King / Clavicula Salomonis (King Solomon and S.L MacGregor Mathers, published by Weiser Books, 1st Paper Edition, 1989, ISBN 978-0877286981)

24. The Love Poems of Rumi (by Jalal al-Din Rumi and Deepak Chopra, published by Harmony Books 1998, ISBN 0609602438)

25. The Method of Handling the Three Ones: A Taoist Manual of Meditation of the Fourth Century A.D. (Andersen, Paul, Curzon Press, 1980, ISBN: 9780700701131)

26. The Philosophy of Hegel (by Georg Wilhelm Friedrich Hegel, published by Random House, Incorporated 1965, ISBN 0394309766)

27. The Road To Reality (by Roger Penrose, published by Random House Inc., 2004, ISBN 0-679-45443-8)

28. The Rosary of the Philosophers (by Adam McLean, published by Phanes Print 1995, ISBN 978-0933999305)

29. The Secret of the Golden Flower (by Lu Dong Bin, translated by Richard Wilhelm, Foreword by C.G. Jung, publisher A Harvest HBJ Book 1962, ISBN 0-15-679980-4)

30. The Special and the General Theory of Relativity (by Albert Einstein, Lawson, Robert W., Dover Publications 2001, 048641714X)

31. The Sum of Perfection or of the Perfect Magistery (by Jabir Ibn Hayyan, published by Kessinger Publishing, LLC, 2010, ISBN 978-1161600476)

32. The Timeless Way of Building (by Cristopher Alexander, published by Oxford University Press, 1979, ISBN 978-0195024029)

33. The Yellow Court Classic history:

http://www.hudong.com/wiki//魏华存

34. The Yoga Sutras of Patanjali (by Swami Vivekananda, publisher: Better World Books 2007, ISBN 9781844834617)

35. What is life (by Erwin Schrödinger, published by Cambridge University Press, 1967, ISBN 052109397X)

36. Wholeness and The Implicate Order (by David Bohm, publisher: Routledge & Kegan Paul 1980, ISBN 0-415-28979-3)

37. Wudang Tao, Member Library (by Master Yun Xiang Tseng and associates), at http://wudangtao.com

38. Yellow Court Scripture (Calligraphy by Wang Xizhi, public domain images referenced at http://wikipedia.org/wiki/File:Wang_Xizhi_Huang_Ting_Jing.jpg)

39. Yellow Emperor Medicine Classic (by Huang Di, translated by Ilza Veith, publisher: University of California Press 1972, ISBN 0-520-02158-4)

40. Yi Jing (translated by Richard Wilhelm, foreword by C.G. Jung, publisher: Routledge & Kegan Paul 1931, ISBN 0-7100-9527-9)